Born in 1909 in Warchau, Eberhard Bethge attended the universities of Königsberg, Berlin, Wien,
Tübingen and Halle. From 1935 to 1940 he was
Assistant to Dietrich Bonhoeffer at the Church
College of Finkenwalde and other places. In 1953
he came to London as Pastor of the Germans in
London where he remained until 1961, apart from
a year (1957–58) which he spent as Visiting Lec-
turer at Harvard Divinity School. He was awarded
the Honorary Degree of D.D. at Glasgow
University in 1962, of Berlin University in 1967,
and of Berne in 1975. In 1961 he became Director
of the Institute of Continuing Education for
Ministers of the Evangelical Church of the
Rhineland at Rengsdorf, until his retirement in
1975. In 1966 he went as Visiting Professor to
Chicago Theological Seminary and in 1967 as
Fosdick Professor to Union Theological
Seminary, New York.

A close friend of Dietrich Bonhoeffer's, he is
editor of the German edition of Bonhoeffer's *Collected Works*, edited his *Ethics* and *Letters and
Papers from Prison*, and is author of *Bonhoeffer:
Exile and Martyr* as well as of the definitive bio-
graphy *Dietrich Bonhoeffer: Theologian, Christian,
Contemporary*.

Eberhard Bethge is married to Dietrich Bonhoeffer's niece, Renate *née* Schleicher.

*This book was written in
co-operation with my wife,
Renate*

COSTLY GRACE

An Illustrated Biography of Dietrich Bonhoeffer

by

EBERHARD BETHGE

Translated by Rosaleen Ockenden

HARPER & ROW, PUBLISHERS

SAN FRANCISCO

Cambridge
Hagerstown
Philadelphia
New York

1817

London
Mexico City
Sao Paolo
Sydney

Grateful acknowledgement is made to
Macmillan Publishing Co. for use of copyrighted material
from Dietrich Bonhoeffer's *Letters and Papers from Prison*, 1972,
and *The Cost of Discipleship*, 1963.

First published in German as DIETRICH BONHOEFFER
by Rowohlt Taschenbuch Verlag GmbH, 1976
in the series "Rowohlts Monographien"
First published in English by
Fount Paperbacks, London and by
Harper & Row, New York, 1979.

Original German edition © Rowohlt Taschenbuch Verlag GmbH, 1976
English translation © William Collins Sons & Co., Ltd.,
London, and Harper & Row, Publishers, Inc., New York, 1979

The text of this book is printed on 100% recycled paper.

FIRST U.S. EDITION

International Standard Book Number: 0-06-060773-4

Library of Congress Catalog Card Number: 78-19492

80 81 82 83 84 10 9 8 7 6 5 4 3 2 1

Contents

London, July 1939

1 *Perspectives*

Anna Morawska the Polish publicist from the Catholic ZNAK group, who died not long ago, said in a talk: "Bonhoeffer is exciting because he dared face the problem of our time, the problem of how to meet Christ when people have become religionless. What relationship do we have with Christ if, in the midst of atheism, we do not wish to see ourselves as agnostics, but are conscious of a reverence for him? If we simply feel that the distinction between so-called believers and so-called unbelievers is a false one? Bound by his middle-class origins and deeply conscious of his cultural heritage, Bonhoeffer, like us today, was not prepared for profound revolutions. Yet precisely because of this, he was ready to make great changes."

In an essay for members of the conspiracy Dietrich Bonhoeffer wrote: "It remains an experience of inestimable value that for once we have learned to see the great events of world history from below, from the perspective of the excluded, the suspected, the ill-treated, the powerless, the oppressed and despised, in short, the suffering. If only no bitterness or envy has gnawed at our hearts at such a time, so that we can see the great things and the small, happiness and misery, strength and weakness with new eyes, so that our perception of the significant, of humanity, justice and mercy has become clearer, freer and less corruptible; so that personal suffering becomes a more useful key, a more fruitful principle for viewing and actively understanding the world than personal happiness. It is only a question of not allowing these perspectives from below to become a prop for the eternally dissatisfied, but instead doing justice to life and giving our assent to it in all its dimensions from a higher contentment which has its true source beyond all concepts of above and below."[1]

In Eastern Europe Bonhoeffer is eagerly studied because

of this forthright attitude to the situation of the view from below; in the West he is the subject of approving or disparaging discussion, chiefly because of fifty pages of theology which he wrote while in prison at Tegel. As an English theologian wrote recently, these pages "have exercised an influence on contemporary religious thought, which is quite out of proportion to their scope and which is all the more surprising when one reflects how much of this thinking has remained fragmentary."[2]

Bonhoeffer, moreover, became a martyr in a German concentration camp because of a political conspiracy. There are certainly contemporary theologians whose work has reached a more perfect systematic completion; but they died a natural death. And there are Christians whose protest against the idolatry of the Hitler era ended in a martyrdom more in line with the Church's traditional preconceptions; but they did not leave behind them stimulating written theology.

The work of Bonhoeffer's which we do possess is incomplete. First we have the early theological books, which are sometimes difficult to read, and which have been published in many languages; then the documents relating to conflicts within the Church and the political struggle; finally the late fragments from Tegel. We are left with the picture of an active life that ended, after thirty-nine years, at the hand of the executioner.

The elements of this life and work form a bridge between hostile blocs and countries, and between divided churches. The influence is one which began to make itself felt only after Bonhoeffer's death. Ten years later there were enquiries about him and his work from all over the world.

It is a remarkable phenomenon, for during his lifetime Bonhoeffer did not particularly bother about publicity.

The final years of his life, and his end, took place in total obscurity. In 1945 men like Niemöller, Wurm, Dibelius and Lilje were known throughout the world. Only the innermost circles had heard of Bonhoeffer, fighter for the

Church, ecumenist and author of *The Cost of Discipleship*.

Who was he, we ask, and mean by the question, what was his life like? Who is he, we ask, and mean by that question, what influence does his work continue to have now?

Gustave Flaubert maintained: *"L'homme, c'est rien, l'œuvre c'est tout"* (The man is nothing; the work is all). We are about to repudiate the comment and, in fact, almost reverse his assertion. The fact that Bonhoeffer's work is incomplete is part of its fascination. His nature remains undiscovered unless he is encountered as a person. He himself accepted the truncated nature of his vocation and writing as his destiny: "The longer we are uprooted from our professional activities and our private lives, the more it brings home to us how fragmentary our lives are compared with those of our parents . . . What chance have any of us today of producing a real *magnum opus*? How can we do all the research, the assimilation and sorting out of material which such a thing entails? . . . That means that culture has become a torso. The important thing today, however, is that people should be able to discern from the fragment of our life how the whole was arranged and planned. For there are some fragments which are only worth throwing into the dustbin, and even a decent hell is far too good for them. But there are other fragments whose importance lasts for centuries, because their completion can only be a matter for God, and therefore they are fragments which must be fragments. I think for example of the Art of the Fugue. If our life is but the remotest reflection of such a fragment. if in a short time we accumulate a wealth of themes and weld them together into a pleasing harmony and keep the great counterpoint going all through . . . then let us not bemoan the fragmentariness of our life, but rather rejoice in it."[3]

In the summer of 1944 he answered the question "Who was Bonhoeffer?" in a poem. Implicit in it lie his origins, the power of his influence, his setbacks and his piety:

WHO AM I?

Who am I? They often tell me
I stepped from my cell's confinement
Calmly, cheerfully, firmly,
Like a squire from his country-house.

Who am I? They often tell me
I used to speak to my warders
Freely and friendly and clearly,
As though it were mine to command.

Who am I? They also tell me
I bore the days of misfortune
Equably, smilingly, proudly,
Like one accustomed to win.

Am I then really all that which other men tell of?
Or am I only what I myself know of myself? —
Restless and longing and sick, like a bird in a cage,
Struggling for breath, as though hands were compressing
  my throat,
Yearning for colours, for flowers, for the voices of birds,
Thirsting for words of kindness, for neighbourliness,
Tossing in expectation of great events,
Powerlessly trembling for friends at an infinite distance,
Weary and empty at praying, at thinking, at making,
Faint, and ready to say farewell to it all?

Who am I? This or the other?
Am I one person today and tomorrow another
Am I both at once? A hypocrite before others,
And before myself a contemptibly woebegone weakling?
Or is something within me still like a beaten army,
Fleeing in disorder from victory already achieved?

Who am I? They mock me, these lonely questions of
  mine,
Whoever I am, Thou knowest, O God, I am Thine![4]

2 *Childhood*

In America, after a lecture on Bonhoeffer the question was once asked: "Dietrich Bonhoeffer must have had a very great influence on his family, how did this influence show itself in practice?" The audience was amazed to hear that his seven brothers and sisters influenced Bonhoeffer at least as much as he influenced them, and that for all eight children their parents were the predominant influence in their lives. People had imagined him as a hero who played the part of a world reformer inside as well as outside the family. In Bonhoeffer's case it is certain that the family influence went far beyond what is usual. This large family had a rare solidarity and his parents' house, with its open, generous hospitality, was and remained a formative centre not only for the immediate family but also for more distant relatives and many like-minded friends.

The Bonhoeffer children, from right to left:
Karl-Friedrich, Walter, Klaus, Ursula, Christine, Dietrich, Sabine.
Breslau, 1908

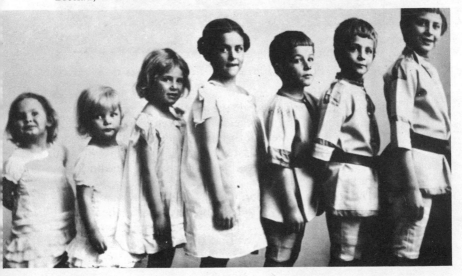

The Father, Professor Karl Bonhoeffer. Christmas 1925

Dietrich Bonhoeffer was born on 4 February 1906 in Breslau, the sixth child in the family, and he had a twin sister, Sabine. The three eldest children were sons: Karl-Friedrich and Walter, both born in 1899, and Klaus born in 1901. Then followed Ursula and Christine in 1902 and 1903. After the twins the youngest child, Susanne, was born in 1909.

Their father, Karl Bonhoeffer, was Professor of Psychiatry and Neurology. In 1912 he was offered the chair at the University of Berlin, the most highly-regarded chair in the subject in Germany at that time, and it was from here that his name became known outside Germany. It is certain that Karl Bonhoeffer was chiefly responsible for the fact that the psychoanalysis of Freud and Jung had difficulty in making an impression in the Berlin Faculty at that period. His colleague Robert Gaupp, who held the chair at Heidelberg, offered the following explanation: "It may perhaps seem striking that a man who was a sensitive psychiatrist with a remarkable gift for empathy and who did outstanding work on the nature of hysterical symptom formation, never, so far as I know, took up a more specific and categorical position in the controversy about the theories of Freud, Adler, Jung and other 'psychoanalysts'. Psychoanalysis means dispassionate analysis of an individual's mental illness with all the resources of empathic psychology and with exact observation. In this empathic psychology and exact observation Bonhoeffer had no superior. But he belonged to the Wernicke school, which was solely orientated on the brain and permitted no departure from thinking in terms of cerebral pathology . . . Intuition was not alien to him, as his whole life's work shows. But he had no urge to advance into the realm of dark, undemonstrable, bold and imaginative interpretation where so much has to be assumed and so little can be proved . . ."[5]

Dietrich Bonhoeffer never really dealt with Freud in any detail, and this was doubtless due mainly to his father's influence.

Karl Bonhoeffer was a man of authority, both to his assistants and students in the Charité, the Berlin University Clinic, as well as at home. He spoke quietly and infrequently, but what he said was noted. Praise and blame were given sparingly but to the point. He gave the impression of self-control and expected the same from his children. Objectivity and balance were his distinguishing characteristics. He abhorred fancy phrases; all the children had to express themselves pertinently and as clearly and concisely as possible, without circumlocutions. The children gained in judgement from this, but certainly developed some inhibitions too. Later Dietrich Bonhoeffer was to

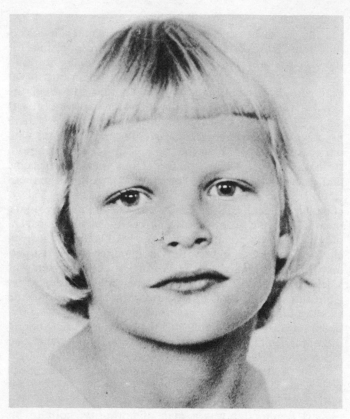

Dietrich, 1913

write: "Many people are spoilt by being satisfied with
mediocrity. It may mean that many get results more
quickly, for they have fewer inhibitions to overcome. I have
found it one of the most potent educative factors in our
family that we have had so many inhibitions to overcome
(I mean, such obstacles as lack of relevance, clarity, natu-
ralness, tact, simplicity, etc.) before we could express freely
what is in our minds . . . It often takes a long time to leap
over such hurdles as these, and one is apt to feel that one
could have achieved success with greater ease and less cost

if these obstacles could have been avoided ... But one never falls short as regards something one has worked to make one's own independently. This is inconvenient for others and sometimes even perhaps for oneself, but these are after all the inconveniences of education ..."[6]

It was at the rather formal mealtimes, when they only spoke if they were spoken to, that the children mainly saw their father. At weekends, on birthdays and during the holidays, he was able to be with them totally. He was known for his complete reliability when he had made a promise. He kept to his daily schedule punctiliously even when most hard-pressed with work. He was always home for a meal at two o'clock. If he held consultations at home in the afternoon, absolute quiet and consideration was demanded from the children. Their father's study was sacrosanct and could be entered, if at all, only with their mother's express permission. Karl Bonhoeffer was a Swabian. The Bonhoeffer family had been emigrants from Holland (van den Boenhoff from Nijmegen) who had settled in Schwäbisch-Hall in 1513. There are still some memorial stones in Hall church, and on some of the houses can be seen the Bonhoeffer coat of arms, granted in 1590: a lion holding a beanpole in his paw. Dietrich Bonhoeffer used to wear a signet ring bearing this coat of arms.

Dietrich Bonhoeffer's grandfather, Friedrich Bonhoeffer, the first member of the family to move away from Hall, became President of the State Court in Ulm. He was a man of great modesty, averse to any ostentation, and an ardent nature-lover and naturalist.

His wife, Dietrich's grandmother, Julie Tafel before her marriage, played an important part in Dietrich's life. She died in 1936 at the age of nearly ninety-four. There was a revolutionary streak in the Tafel family, who were also Swabian. Some of the family had been expelled from Württemberg as members of a national liberal fraternity and democrats, one emigrated and another became a follower of Swedenborg. Julie had a critical mind and a determined character. She took part in the movement for

15

The Grandmother, Julie Bonhoeffer, *née* Tafel (1842–1936)

women's emancipation and was opposed to Hitler from the beginning. When on 1 April 1933 SA guards were posted in front of the Berlin department store of the West, during the boycott of Jewish businesses, it did not stop her from going into the shop.

Dietrich's mother Paula (*née* von Hase) came of a Prussian family. Her father, Karl-Alfred, had been chaplain at the court of William II, but resigned his post after a disagreement with the Emperor. He became a member of the Supreme Church Council and professor of practical theology. His life was greatly influenced by the example of his father, the well-known church and dogmatic historian from Jena, Karl-August von Hase. His mother was

16

The Mother, Paula Bonhoeffer, *née* von Hase. Christmas 1925

Pauline Härtel, one of the daughters of the Leipzig music publisher.

Although Dietrich never knew his maternal grandmother, Clara von Hase, *née* Countess Kalckreuth, her family tradition was an important element in the Bonhoeffer family life. Clara was very musical and had studied the piano under Franz Liszt and Clara Schumann. For the Kalckreuths art was even more important than music for Stanislaus, Clara's father, had broken with the military tradition of the family and became a painter. Pictures by him hang in the Pinakothek Gallery in Munich, and works by his son Leopold in the Hamburg Kunsthalle. The Bonhoeffers naturally had many paintings by the two Kalck-

17

reuths, as well as by their teachers, friends and pupils, such as Lenbach and Achenbach.

Paula, for long the youngest of the Hase children, was optimistic and sociable by temperament, lively, imaginative and energetic; for her there was no such thing as an insoluble problem. As a child and young girl she would at times impetuously overstep the bounds of conventional etiquette. She fought successfully, for instance, for the right to take the qualifying examination as a teacher.

The Christian education she had herself received was important to her, and in her own way she saw that it was handed on. The Church did not play a large part in her life, although this altered later when the Confessing Church was the only institution to show any real resistance to the Hitler regime. She made sure, however, that the children knew the Bible and the hymns that she herself cherished. In their early years she taught the elder children herself, together with other children of the same age belonging to friends in the neighbourhood; the younger children had a governess, except for religious instruction, which she gave them herself.

The principal aim of the upbringing she gave the children was to make them responsible human beings. She saw that upbringing as having a Christian value and her husband saw it as having a humanist one. The guidelines which sprang from this aim were naturally not always made explicit, but they were a natural part of the Bonhoeffer family life and of the lives of their friends.

Consideration for the needs and feelings of others was expected of the children from an early age, and their parents' praise or blame was concentrated almost exclusively on this area. Such consideration for others became an important element in Dietrich Bonhoeffer's theology.

Such a standard of behaviour demanded a great deal from the children, but it also gave them security. Since they were bound to take others seriously, they were sure of being taken seriously themselves and of having their own opinions respected. None the less these same high stan-

18

In Wölfelsgrund, 1910

dards called forth several often wittily expressed criticisms of others, and could also cause them anxieties when they left the family circle to go into a world in which such standards were no longer valid.

The parents placed great emphasis on the fact that the children should have freedom of movement and that each child should develop according to his particular talents. Torn clothes or broken windows were not regarded as important. The children had ample space at home and their governesses were carefully chosen to make sure that real consideration was given to each child. Their mother had a great deal of imagination and arranged lively parties for the grown-ups as well as the children, and provided a constant series of amusements in the form of games, stories, dramatic productions and expeditions.

Each child had lessons either in singing or on the piano, the violin or the cello. On Saturdays the family gathered for a musical evening, either to play together or to listen to anything new that one of the children had learned. Dietrich early became a good pianist; he accompanied his mother and also his brothers and sisters, and his achievement was such that by the time he was fourteen he and his parents thought that he might train as a professional pianist. As an adult too he played the piano a great deal and was especially fond of chamber music, which he often played with his brother-in-law, Rüdiger Schleicher, and his brother Klaus, who played the violin and cello. In the last few years before he was sent to prison, he discovered the songs of Hugo Wolf and used sometimes to accompany Eberhard Bethge on the piano. The sacred songs of Heinrich Schütz were another discovery. In the most turbulent times of resistance and war, they would spend an hour or two every day making music together, and often the whole family would join in practising Schütz cantatas at the Schleichers' house.

Although the Bonhoeffer home was run on a lavish scale, care was taken not to spoil the children. They were expected to go a good distance on foot to save their tram or streetcar money. They had to keep precise accounts of their pocket money and it was Klaus who hit upon the idea of entering anything missing under the heading of "charity".

From a modern standpoint their upbringing was probably "authoritarian", since the parents' word was never questioned, but by the standards of the time it was fairly liberal. The parents tried to start from the child's point of view and to make up for any lack he might feel. They had a sense of humour and knew how to overlook a child's misdemeanours, but expected in their turn that any child

The twins Dietrich and Sabine, 1915

In the professorial quarter of Berlin-Grunewald:
Wangenheimstr. 14

The living room

would be able to take small injustices in his stride without feeling sorry for himself. At the same time it was clear to the children that they had to fight against real injustice, whether it affected themselves or other people.

The values in which Bonhoeffer was brought up form the background of his *Ethics*.

*

Berlin was and remained for Bonhoeffer the decisive city: imperial, republican, and then reluctantly national socialist Berlin; liberal, ecclesiastical, conservative and cosmopolitan Berlin, with its academic and working-class areas, its concert halls and museums; the Berlin of street-fighting and, later, of conspiracy.

For four years the family lived in the Brückenallee, close to the Tiergarten. Then they moved into the Grunewald district, to the house at 14 Wangenheimstrasse, where they lived until 1935.

It was a district of academics. The physicist Max Planck lived nearby, as well as the theologian Adolf von Harnack, the medical specialists His and Hertwig, and the historian Hans Delbrück.

Klaus Bonhoeffer became close friends with Justus, one of the Delbrück sons, and later married his sister Emmi.

Through the new school, the classical grammar school at Grunewald, the children made new friendships, such as that with the Dohnanyi family. Later two of them married two Bonhoeffers: Hans von Dohnanyi married Christine and Grete von Dohnanyi married Karl-Friedrich. Gerhard Leibholz, who was of Jewish descent, was drawn into this circle of friends through confirmation classes and later married Sabine. Dietrich soon joined the group, although he was younger, and his ties with it remained strong even later in life; indeed his fate was finally determined by these bonds of friendship.

It was wartime when the family moved to the Wangen-heimstrasse. Karl Bonhoeffer has recorded his impressions of those days in his memoirs: "We did not really believe

23

that there was going to be a war, even though the encircle-
ment by the Triple Entente was felt to be alarming. All the
same, I remember having been given the disquieting feeling, in the company of some staff officers in the winter of
1913–14, that the possibility of an early armed clash must
be taken into account . . . One particular memory of those
agitated days that remains in my mind is that of the evening of the day the British declared war, when we and the
three boys were on the Unter den Linden. The earlier
enthusiasm of the crowds in the street and in front of
the castle and the government buildings had yielded to a
gloomy silence, which made the scene extraordinarily oppressive."[7]

In his New Year notes in 1916 Karl Bonhoeffer wrote:
"Today we await the inevitably negative answer of the
Entente. The American peace proposal, which followed
ours, is regarded with suspicion since we fear America's
interference in any sort of peace negotiations, because of
her strong ties with England . . . It is impossible to form an
independent judgement from a censored press and impossible not to be disturbed by the political events which
appear to spring from a lack of organic purpose. The
constant appeal to the good sense of the subject, who is
only permitted retrospective considerations, has nothing
edifying about it."[8]

During this period cousins of the Bonhoeffer children
were killed in action or severely wounded. In 1917 two of
the brothers, Karl-Friedrich and Walter, enlisted as vol-
unteers. On 23 April Walter was wounded, and on 28
April, three hours before his death, he dictated his last
letter from the field hospital: "My dear family, today I had
the second operation, which I must admit was far less
pleasant because deeper fragments were removed . . . My
technique of letting my thoughts bypass the pain had to be
put into practice here too. But there are more interesting
things in the world than my wound. The possible consequence of Mount Kemmel and today's news of the taking
of Ypres give us great cause for hope. I dare not think

In the Grunewald High School, 1920/21.
Dietrich, fourth from right

about my poor regiment, so severely has it suffered in the last few days. How are things going with the other officer cadets? I think of you all, you dear ones, and long to see you again every minute of the long days and nights. Yours so far away, Walter."[9]

His mother seemed broken by his death and it was a long time before she recovered from the blow. For ten years his father made no further entries in the New Year note book, which he had kept punctiliously up until then.

His brother's death and his mother's agonized grief had a profound effect upon Dietrich, who was twelve years old at the time.

Klaus, who was by then seventeen, was also called up briefly at the end of the war.

*

These wartime experiences no doubt played a part in Dietrich's decision to become a pastor and theologian. He was perhaps also influenced in choosing his career by the fact that he was entering a totally different field from his bro-

25

thers and that he, the youngest, would be able to make his mark independently. His decision was finally made when, in his penultimate year at school, he chose Hebrew as his optional subject. He was then fifteen years old.

His father wanted him to make his own decision and held back his own views. Later on he wrote to him: "When you made up your mind to study theology, I sometimes could not help thinking that it would be a pity for you to have the quiet, uneventful life of a minister, such as I knew my Swabian uncles had and such as Mörike describes. As far as its being uneventful is concerned, I was greatly mistaken. I had no conception, with my scientific background, that nowadays there could be such a crisis in the ecclesiastical sphere too."[10] His mother's attitude to Dietrich's decision to take up the same vocation as her own father and grandfather was certainly a less negative one.

The richness of talents and interests in the extended family circle ensured that there was no danger of Dietrich's decision leading to a narrowing of his horizons, as is often thought to happen among theologians. His unusually close relationship with his brothers and sisters and in-laws meant that he always knew a great deal about the worlds in which they lived. The conversations and exchange of information did not stop even in later years, when all Dietrich's energy was devoted to working for the Church.

His three brothers had an aptitude for science. Karl-Friedrich, an agnostic, who later became a professor of physics and gained an international reputation in the field of hydrogen chemistry and reaction kinetics, was especially sensitive and warm-hearted. Dietrich later talked a great deal to him about church problems, and his birthday letters to him are important biographical sources. Klaus, the most difficult, amusing and, according to his father, the most gifted of the eight children, had intended to become a doctor but in fact found his career in law. They travelled a great deal together, which Dietrich enjoyed because of the fascination Klaus felt for exotic places and sights. Walter had a detailed knowledge of forests and animals and had also written some surprising poetry. After Walter's death Dietrich was given his confirmation Bible, which he used for his own meditations all his life. Ursula undertook social and educational studies under Anna von Gierke; her husband, Rüdiger Schleicher, who was a lawyer, was one of Dietrich's most frequent companions in lively philosophical and theological discussion or in English conversation. Christine studied biology; her husband, Hans von Dohnanyi, was Dietrich's most constant source of information first about the political world, then about the world of the conspiracy. His twin sister, Sabine, went to an art school; Dietrich's association with her husband, Gerhard Leibholz, a constitutional lawyer, was to grow even deeper in the years that followed; later, when Gerhard was in exile, George Bell, Bishop of Chichester, extended to him the friendship he had shown to Dietrich.[11] His youngest sister, Susanne, shared his interest in the Church and theology, and helped him with the children's services he arranged in Grunewald; the man she later married, Walter Dress, studied church history with Dietrich at the theological faculty in Berlin, as a graduate student.

The broad spectrum of influences and opportunities which had determined the pattern of his childhood and youth was widened further by such connections. The youthful enthusiasm for amateur theatricals – Dietrich had himself written a play based on Wilhelm Hauff's fairy-tale "The Cold Heart" – was turned to producing plays for performance on the eve of family weddings. Years later in his prison cell his early passion for playing chess helped him to pass the time by working out theories of the game.

The Bonhoeffers read a lot as a family. Dietrich caught the habit of reading the classics from his elder brothers before they could be spoiled for him by compulsory study at school. In Tegel prison he returned to the world of nineteenth-century writing, which was a favourite with his family. He notes: "In my reading I am now concentrating entirely on the nineteenth century. During recent months I have read Gotthelf, Stifter, Immermann, Fontane and Keller with sheer admiration. A period in which people could write such clear and simple German must have had quite a healthy core. They treat the most delicate matters without sentimentality, the most serious without flippancy, and they express their convictions without pathos; there is no exaggerated simplifying or complicating of language or subject matter; in short, it is all very much to my liking".[12]

In his last year at school he was already reading Friedrich Naumann and Max Weber with interest, spurred on by his elder brothers and his brother-in-law, Rüdiger Schleicher. Naumann's analysis left a permanent sting in the tail: "Many people are in practical terms money merchants with the right hand and benefactors of the poor with the left . . . All the exhortations of the Gospel float like distant white clouds of yearning over all the real action of our time."[13] He was later passionately to rebel against this over-neat distinction drawn between what is relevant and irrelevant, between world and Gospel.

He was as yet not particularly excited by theological problems. None the less, he had his own copy of Schleiermacher's *Talks on Religion* and Eduard Meyer's *Birth and Origins of Christianity* and read both while still in his last year at school. Yet for his Abitur school-leaving examination he chose as his optional subject to write an essay on literature of a totally different sort: "Catullus and Horace as Lyrical Poets".

3   The Years of Study

At university in Tübingen Dietrich joined the students'
fraternity called the "Hedgehog". His fellow students describe him as capable and assured in manner, stormy in
temperament, receptive to new ideas, inclined to indulge
in teasing, and endowed with a sharp critical sense, which
he was, however, equally prepared to turn towards himself.

His first steps towards independence, away from the all-
pervasive norms of his parents' home, seem to have been
virtually free of problems. His eagerness for a new life and
for his studies more than outweighed any anxieties about
the demands which would be made on him.

He wrote weekly letters home, however. Every decision
that had to be made about choice of lectures, buying
books (a real problem in those days of ever-increasing in-
flation), joining the students' union, even the most trivial
of arrangements was reported, carefully considered and
parental approval sought. Only one decision was made
hastily: to take part in an exercise organized by the "Black
Reichswehr" in Ulm. He wrote to his parents anxiously
afterwards, justifying his decision and asking for their approval and consent.

As he had chosen his vocation freely so in the same way
he organized his studies independently. He wrote: "The
lectures this semester are almost all particularly attractive
in my field, so I am kept in college practically the whole
day."[14]

Dietrich Bonhoeffer's initial time in Tübingen showed
all the characteristics of an academic study of theology
and scarcely any signs of a real commitment to the
Church. His parents probably thought that this would
remain so. With the impartiality typical of a first-semester
student, he put his name down for a great deal of philos-

29

As a student in Tübingen

ophy. The philosopher Karl Groos, who in 1923 was working on the problems of epistemology, was the only professor whose lectures Bonhoeffer attended during both his
semesters at Tübingen. He did not do so for those of either
Karl Heim or Adolf Schlatter, who were at the time the
best-known theologians in Tübingen. Under Groos the
seventeen-year-old worked on a paper on Kant's *Critique
of Pure Reason*. Schlatter attracted him too, however, and
next to Luther became the exegete he used most. Karl
Heim, who provided him with his first practical introduction to Schleiermacher's *Talks on Religion*, was a dogma-
tist whom he later came to regard more and more critically. During his time as a student at Tübingen Bonhoeffer
had not as yet read anything by Karl Barth that might
have attracted him, in spite of the fact that precisely in
1923 the whole theological world was discussing a sharp
correspondence between Barth, then a young university

lecturer at Göttingen, and Adolf von Harnack, the Nestor of Berlin. Their exchange of views on the poor future ahead for theology and the Church, for which each held the other responsible, was published in *Christliche Welt*. Bonhoeffer was at the time absorbed in the history of religion and was studying textual criticism as practised by the Tübingen exegetes. He also attended "general studies", for instance on "Form in Beethoven's Symphonies", and took part in his student association's debates on social and political questions.

The Hedgehog was a Swabian fraternity, founded in 1871, of liberal views and leaning towards Bismarck – a feasible combination at that time. The fraternity's headquarters were on the heights overlooking the Neckar just behind the old castle. In contrast to the affectations of older, colour-carrying and duelling fraternities, they wore the dull, bristly hedgehog skin on their heads. But eventually the Hedgehog too adopted certain "codes of honour" and in 1933 it, like the others, inserted the Aryan clause in its constitution. In 1933 Dietrich Bonhoeffer left the fraternity. His elder brothers had never felt able to join it while they were students, even though both their father and their uncle had been members. (Rudolf Bultmann was also a member.) Karl-Friedrich had protested against nationalistic pressure on members of the students' associations in 1919, when they were used in the suppression of risings in Stuttgart and Munich. Dietrich, however, at the time less inclined to the left politically than his brothers, felt a need for the company of young men of his own age. They had found it during their military service, and he found it here in the fraternity. At that time the members took part in social work, discussion about Friedrich Naumann, and vacation work in the Ruhr. "In fact, I found I liked the people fairly well",[15] he wrote home. It was the first time he had formed a group of friends outside the circle of family contacts. In later years the period in the Hedgehog was forgotten completely and with remarkable rapidity.

Adolf von Harnack

Later he talked occasionally about one episode which he owed to his membership of the Hedgehog: the two weeks of military training with the Ulm Rifles. In 1923 both right and left wings armed and trained for possible clashes, particularly on the eastern frontiers. In the provinces groups hostile to the constitution formed and stockpiled weapons. It was the time of the *putsch* (revolt) by Ludendorff and Hitler. In Saxony there were disorders inspired by the Communists. After the French occupation of the Ruhr further attacks from the East were feared. The Reich government made preparations with the High Command of the 100,000 strong army; the army commanders-in-chief approved the illegal training of students in short exercises, before the Allied Control Commission could keep up a sharper watch or call a halt to them. Many of the Tübingen students left the lecture rooms for several weeks. Dietrich wrote home: "At first I said it was impossible, but that I would go some time during the vacation. But, when I was told that from 1 December onwards training was to be supervised by the Entente Control Commission, I reconsidered the matter ... now I think it better to get it over and done with as quickly as possible, so as to have the assurance of being able to help in the event of critical situations."[16] He felt satisfaction in standing up to the service and the rough conditions without any difficulty, although he was disturbed by what he observed: "The Reichswehr teams on the whole make a good impression, but nearly all of them are very reactionary... They are all awaiting the moment when Ludendorff will do the thing with better (that is, with Reichswehr) support [better than in Hitler's *putsch* of 9 November 1923]. Their attitude contrasts completely with that of the people here in the house [the Hedgehog students' fraternity house] who would all like to kill Ludendorff."[17] At this period, 1923, he and his brothers read the Social Democrat newspaper *Vorwärts* in the family holiday house at Friedrichsbrunn in the eastern Harz mountains.

The Ulm interlude was Bonhoeffer's only experience of military life in uniform.

*

The final brief term he spent in Rome seems to have had far more influence on Bonhoeffer than the entire year in Tübingen. Suddenly the Church as a phenomenon entered his field of vision.

After he had recovered from a serious fall incurred while ice-skating, his parents financed his journey to Rome as an eighteenth birthday present. For Bonhoeffer Rome was not only the ancient city he remembered from his school Latin lessons, but rather that of his famous great-grandfather Carl von Hase, who had spent some time there with Gregorovius, Hildebrand and Thorvaldsen and also with their opposite numbers, the cardinals and archbishops of the First Vatican Council of 1869–70. "I knew Baedecker by heart by the time I started on the trip," he wrote in his

Karl Barth

diary. Easter Day in St Peter's made him conscious how nationalistic, provincial and narrow-minded were the confines of his own church. Although he found the audience with the Pope disappointing, for the very first time he was struck by the universality of the Church. This did not prevent him from debating Catholic dogma from a critical Protestant standpoint with a Catholic priest: "... He would very much have liked to convert me ... but this way he is least likely to succeed." None the less he wrote in his diary: "I am beginning, to understand the concept of the Church."

It is from this period that Bonhoeffer's critical love of the larger sister church stems. He began his own independent theological work in his dissertation (*Sanctorum Communio*) with the problem of the Church; not with abstract problems of epistemological definition as such, but with that concrete phenomenon as a fact of sociological as well as theological entity. When his friend Eberhard Bethge passed through Rome in uniform in 1944, Bonhoeffer in his prison cell showered him with advice as to what he should see – not ancient Rome, but rather Catholic Rome.

*

Bonhoeffer returned to Berlin in June 1924, just in time to enrol for a further semester at his home university. He spent the remainder of his time as a student at the Berlin theological faculty, which was well known to be liberal and where the lectures were given by world famous scholars. A new commitment, however, made him critical of his great teachers, Harnack, Karl Holl, the renowned Luther scholar, and Reinhold Seeberg, who was to be his doctoral supervisor. In the winter of 1924–25 he made the most important discovery, theologically, of his life: Karl Barth, who had moved from Göttingen to Münster. The encounter remained for a long time a purely literary one, as it was years before Bonhoeffer sought any personal contact. It signalled, however, the end of the indecision of the first semester; a new certainty about the revelation manifested in the Church guided his studies. He began a passionate search for its concrete form.

None the less, there was no narrowing of his interests. He enrolled for lectures given by non-theologians too, the great men whom Hitler later expelled from Berlin: Heinrich Maier on the theory of epistemology, Wolfgang Köhler on Gestalt theory and Max Wertheimer on psychology. When Adolf von Harnack became an emeritus professor and continued to hold seminars for a select group, Bonhoeffer attended faithfully. In 1925 he began work for his

35

doctorate. He concluded it as he was about to take the
first of his church's theological examinations, and he was
still only twenty-one years old.

In Berlin he enjoyed the exhibitions, the Philharmonia
Orchestra and the choral academy. He watched with
interest his elder brother's work under the tutelage of
Laue, Nernst, Einstein and Planck, and the way in which
the international world of scholarship in East and West
opened up to him. He was little affected as a student by
the political conflicts of the twenties and had only a
sketchy acquaintance with the ideas of Marx and the wor-
kers' movement. It is true that he incorporated a section
on the proletariat in his doctorate, but he allowed Seeburg
to omit it for the printed version.[18] He had little understanding of Expressionism. When his fellow-student
Helmut Rössler read aloud to him Franz Werfel's poems,
he listened with surprise. He had never heard of them before. Like other theologians at that time, Bonhoeffer had
no contact with the great Jewish thinkers: Rosenzweig,
Buber and Baeck. Even Karl Heim was of little use as a
link here, although before the advent of National Socialism
he had been greatly influenced by Buber's work. However,
in the new 1934 edition of his work, all the references to
Buber were omitted!

Every theological student had to provide evidence of
practical parish work for his first examination. During his
final semesters Bonhoeffer took over a children's service in
the Grunewald church. He enjoyed the contact with children enormously. He invited groups of them home and
organized expeditions and games; he took a caring interest
in them as individuals. Later he started discussion groups
with the older ones. It was then that he made the discovery
– at times a frightening one for him – of how easily he
could form a bond with people. He found it uncanny and
worrying.

Whenever Bonhoeffer achieved anything in his life, he
was always acutely aware of his power to influence, his
power over people. Right up to the time of his imprison-

ment he had a deeply rooted fear of what, using the old spiritual concept, he termed his "temptation" towards *accidie*, Luther's biting melancholy of death: the disgust with oneself that lies ever in wait.[19] This disgust – which we shall come across again – arose in his case not from his weaknesses but from his strengths.

*

Now, when the academic world was open to him, he began to feel the attraction of the pulpit more than that of a university chair. He decided to start training for the Church. The training began with two years as a curate in a parish and then after a second examination in theology led to ordination. It not only took him into a completely un-accustomed milieu, but aroused in him a characteristic enthusiasm for testing theory in practice. Suddenly he no longer felt responsible merely for himself and his private circle but for strangers too, and for his actions and words within a wider, albeit still small, public sphere.

In February 1928 Bonhoeffer began his year as assistant pastor to the German Protestant business community in the busy Spanish port of Barcelona. He wrote: "Here one comes into contact with the strangest people, with whom one would not normally have exchanged a single word: bums, vagabonds, criminals fleeing from justice, many foreign legionaries, lion-tamers and animal-trainers who have absconded from the Krone circus on its Spanish tour, German dancers from the local music-halls, German mur-derers on the run ... We are constantly arranging pas-sages home for Germans, even though we know the situa-tion is no better there."

Dietrich Bonhoeffer devoted himself completely to the community life of the German colony with its choir and tennis club. He wrote in his diary that visits to his parish-ioners' homes were "very pleasant, but the conversation is quite different from what one is used to at home. I have not had a single conversation of the Berlin–Grunewald type since I have been here." The fact of being subordinate to an ordinary minister and dependent upon an easily satisfied circle of young and old in no way dampened his eagerness to organize new groups. He got on well with the minister, whose main reading was "nationalistic literature and newspapers", as he noted in his diary. "Since I was only staying for a year I let pass without comment a great deal that I would otherwise have objected to ... Never once in the whole year did we discuss a theological, let alone a religious, problem. Fundamentally we remained strangers, even though we liked one another. He gave me a completely free hand and I am grateful for that." He gained more from bullfighting and its ritual than from his contact with the Spanish Catholic clergy: ". . . horrifyingly uneducated faces . . . a remarkable contrast to Rome. I feel that here there really is some justification for the foolish saying that religion is the opium of the people."[20]

*

Without making any final decision about joining the ministry, Bonhoeffer returned to the academic world of the Berlin theological faculty in the spring of 1929. "I feel that academic work will not hold me for long. But I do think that as thorough an academic grounding as possible is all-important." He intended first of all to finish his habilitation thesis, which would qualify him for entering a university career if he later decided to do so, and he completed it in the shortest possible time, with typical concentration on the goal he had set himself. On 31 July 1930 he gave his inaugural lecture on the demanding theme: "The Question of Man in Contemporary Philosophy and Theology".[21] His habilitation thesis *Act and Being* suffered the same fate in book form as did his doctoral thesis: after grappling with the increased printing costs in a rapidly worsening economic crisis, Bonhoeffer saw the thesis published only to meet with disappointingly little response. At the same time as he was working on the habilitation thesis, he was preparing for the second examination before the Berlin–Brandenburg provincial church, at

the end of his theological training. He was now fully quali-
fied for ordination, but was obliged to wait another year
and a half until he reached the prescribed "canonical" age
of twenty-five. This lent support to a decision to fit in a
year studying abroad. Vital changes were already taking
place in Germany at this time: Stresemann, slandered by
the right as a politician of appeasement, died in 1929; the
New York Stock Exchange collapsed; Joseph Goebbels,
the party propaganda chief, became the Nazi Gauleiter in
Berlin; in 1930 Brüning took over as Chancellor of the
Reich, and the period of government by emergency decree
began. Erik Peterson, who had become a Catholic, wrote
to Harnack: "Spiritually and sociologically the Evangelical
Church corresponds roughly with the mental and sociological status of the German National People's Party."[22]
Bonhoeffer still kept his distance from current affairs, although he now made contact with Barth's friend Günther
Dehn, who as the minister in Moabit was causing uneasiness in church circles by his membership of the SPD
(Social-Democratic Party). "Fendt and Dehn are almost
the only preachers I can really listen to."[23] In the Bonhoeffer home they read the democratic newspaper, the
Vossische Zeitung.

At this point there began a close and later significant
friendship with Franz Hildebrandt, a slightly younger
theologian from a half-Jewish family, who was working on
his doctoral thesis on the Lutheran *est*. They were drawn
to one another not by political activities, although they
both reacted against the right in their views; they were
both inspired by an inexhaustible desire to reach a deeper
understanding of Holy Scripture through the study of
Luther, and by a dissatisfaction with the faculty.

Dietrich Bonhoeffer prepared carefully for his year as
an exchange student in America. He studied the sources on
Allied propaganda against Germany during the First
World War and collected statements about war guilt contained in the famous Article 231 of the Treaty of Versail-
les. He did not, however, need to use the material he gath-

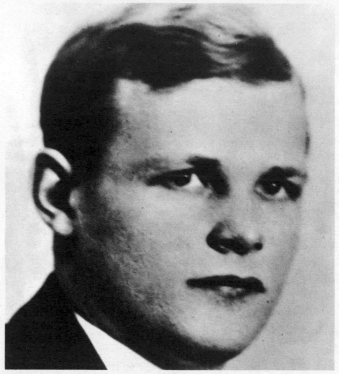
In New York, 1930

ered, for he found that there was a surprisingly friendly attitude to Germany on the other side of the Atlantic, and for the first time he came into contact with a remarkable Christian pacifism.

*

The time that Bonhoeffer spent in Rome and Barcelona had been motivated and largely taken up by cultural concerns. His experiences in New York contained for the first time an ecumenical element.

Dietrich Bonhoeffer's church superior in Berlin, Superintendent Max Diestel, was a supporter of the World Alliance for Friendship Between the Churches (usually

known as the World Alliance), a branch of the new Protestant ecumenical movement, strongly influenced by humanist and American tendencies. Diestel prevailed upon
Bonhoeffer to accept a one-year scholarship at the famous
Union Theological Seminary. Reinhold Niebuhr taught
there, as well as other founder members of the great ecumenical movements. For Bonhoeffer the adventure gave
rise to mixed feelings, composed partly of curiosity and
partly of a feeling of German theological arrogance towards seminaries in the United States, which were ethical
rather than theological in their outlook. He was shocked,
reporting how students had laughed aloud and openly at a
quotation about sin and forgiveness from Luther's famous
treatise, *De servo arbitrio*; it struck them as funny. He
fought passionately for the line of tradition from Paul to
Luther, Kierkegaard and Barth. In one lecture he said: "I
must confess that the only conceivable way in which you
could truly come into contact with his (Barth's) thinking,

Members of Union Theological Seminary. Left to right:
Bonhoeffer, Klemm, Marion Lehmann, Paul Lehmann, Erwin
Sutz. New York, 1931

it seems to me, would be to forget everything you have ever learnt, at least for this one hour."

But he was eager to learn too: to learn about the outward-looking, activist Protestant movement of the "social gospel", about the Behaviourism of William James and John Dewey, about the problems of prohibition and the Depression. Of major importance to him was his encounter with the Negro problem in Harlem, right outside the walls of Union Seminary itself.

As early as 1930 he wrote: "According to the whole mood in contemporary Negro literature, it seems to me that the race question is arriving at a turning-point. The attempt to overcome the conflict religiously or ethically will turn into a violent political confrontation."

He was deeply impressed too by the phenomenon of American church pacificism, despised by the average German Lutheran at the time. Here his friendship with Jean Lasserre, a fellow scholar from France, encouraged and deepened his interest. Lasserre combined a respectable European theology with a simple obedience to the peace teaching contained in the Sermon on the Mount. Bonhoeffer now began to attack the traditional Lutheran separation of the realm of faith and the realm of politics. It became a theological and existential struggle which led him through many stages and which ended with his participation in the conspiracy against Hitler.

In Barcelona Bonhoeffer had conceived the idea of making a journey to India before going home, at that time his principal thought being to experience true Asian piety. Now he dreamed the dream for the second time, but this time his main intention was to study Gandhi's concept of political pacificism at first hand. Again nothing came of it —as was indeed to be the case with his third attempt, from London in 1935. But this recurrent dream played an important part in Bonhoeffer's development. His colleagues at home, Barth included, never understood it properly. Perhaps only at the end of his life did the nature of this attempt become clear: it was the wish to understand his own tradition of Christianity in the light of quite different ways of life and of thinking, and so to find new expression for it.

His return from the United States marked the end of his uncommitted study, writing and observation. The theologian had become more political. During his absence abroad the National Socialists had won their first landslide victories at the polls. He left behind in New York his American friend, Paul Lehmann, who, at a vital moment (1939), was to try once more to turn the course of Bonhoeffer's life away from Germany.

4   *University Lecturer*

In 1931, at the age of twenty-five, Bonhoeffer took on public responsibilities for the first time as a university lecturer. In 1936 he was relieved of his academic post by the National Socialist Minister of Education. He was by then an ordained minister of his church and undertook the dual work of students' chaplain and assistant pastor for his church; he also accepted an official position in the newest international movement in the Church's history, the ecumenical movement, from which as a student he had held himself aloof. (In 1925 Nathan Söderblom had called together in Stockholm the World Conference of the Council for Practical Christianity, Life and Work, in which Berlin professors played a leading part. Bonhoeffer regarded it then as a totally unsatisfactory undertaking theologically.)

So Bonhoeffer took up a mass of duties which must have placed a strain upon even his energies. He gave university lectures and seminars, delivered sermons and talks, prepared candidates for confirmation, travelled and organized international conferences. In fact when he embarked upon his vocation in 1931, this represented a profound and decisive turning-point in his life. His questions changed, they now revolved around the pastoral and ethical authority of the Church. He now had to deal with many people, and at conferences he urged them rather to be silent than to pass premature resolutions. And he had to come to terms with himself too. He attempted to make theological sense of the problem of authority and that of his own power by giving a strong central place in all his work and thinking to Christ who rules and is all-powerful.

Before beginning work in Berlin, he made time for a meeting which meant a great deal to him and which he had always put off – perhaps through shyness, in case his own inner development might be adversely influenced by meeting very strong personalities. He travelled to Bonn to hear Karl Barth during the final weeks of the summer semester. He had been given an introduction by his Swiss friend Erwin Sutz, who had been on a scholarship in New York at the same time as Bonhoeffer himself. He wrote to Sutz: "I have, I think, seldom regretted anything in my theological past so much as the fact that I did not go to him sooner. And now there are only three weeks that I can be here. Lectures, seminars, societies, open evenings and just yesterday a few hours over lunch with Barth . . . it is important and, in the nicest way, astonishing to see there is even more to Barth than his books. He has a frankness, a willingness to listen to criticism, providing that it is relevant, and at the same time such concentration and a violent insistence on the subject whether it is discussed with arrogance or modesty, dogmatically or quite tentatively . . . I am even more impressed by his conversation than by his writings and lectures. Here you really see the whole man. I have never seen anything like it before nor thought anything like it possible."[24]

This was the beginning of a series of intensive meetings which took place either in Berlin or on the Bergli, where Barth had a holiday home. There they would argue about theology on the one hand, and agree about church politics and national politics on the other. In particular, they were united in their support of Barth's friend Günther Dehn, who was increasingly under attack both from students and from church leaders as "a man without a country", after his peace speech at the Barlach war memorial in Magdeburg Cathedral.[25] In 1932 Bonhoeffer used his family connections to put Barth's name forward for Arthur Titius's vacant chair of theology in Berlin, but without success. "I hear you have put yourself out on my behalf," Barth wrote to him. ". . . I would doubtless have accepted . . . the world is in a bad way, but we won't let our pipe go out under any circumstances, will we?"[26] (4 February 1933).

As far as theology was concerned, their differences mostly revolved around Bonhoeffer's fear that the pre-eminence Barth gave to eschatology could blunt the importance of ethics and favour the evasion of real decision, of perhaps the extreme peace commandment.

*

A second event occurred before Bonhoeffer began work which was to prove decisive, both for his life and for his death: his active participation in the ecumenical movement.

His superintendent, Max Diestel, persuaded him to represent Germany at the World Alliance Conference in Cambridge in September 1931. He returned home with a new position, as one of the three secretaries for ecumenical youth work, responsible for central and northern Europe.

In connection with the preparations for the conference there were well-publicised preliminaries in Germany. Professors of theology like Paul Althaus from Erlangen and Emanuel Hirsch from Göttingen published a statement in the *Hamburger Nachrichten* which delighted the right-wing press. In it they said that it had to be admitted "that a Christian and church understanding is impossible, so long as the others conduct against us policies lethal for our nation. Anyone who believes he can serve the cause of understanding today in other ways, denies the German destiny and confuses consciences at home and abroad."[27] So participation in the conference was equivalent to treason. The powerful Evangelische Bund (German Evangelical Alliance) gave its support to the declaration; the church newspaper, the *Allgemeine Lutherische Kirchenzeitung*, opened its columns to the two professors. Bonhoeffer, however,writing to Erwin Sutz about his departure for Cambridge, commented: "What shall we say, after our year in America, about co-operation between the churches? At any rate, not the sort of nonsense that Hirsch talked recently." After Cambridge he said in a report: "The effects of the Cambridge Conference are insignificant in Germany, because nationalistic professors of theology oppose the work of the World Alliance."[28]

After this incursion into ecumenical work – more enforced than voluntary – Bonhoeffer was given the task of co-ordinating efforts in ecumenical youth work within Germany and organizing conferences on a national as well as an international scale. With an almost ruthless intensity he insisted upon thorough theological work at the conferences in England, France, Switzerland and Czechoslovakia. He was in constant disagreement with his Anglo-Saxon colleagues, as he tried to prevent over-hasty resolutions being passed and sought to develop instead a truly ecumenical theology. This all ended abruptly in 1933: from then on it was Bonhoeffer himself who was eager to pass resolutions. But during the period 1931–32 he felt that any statement should be a concrete one and made with the full authority of the theological mandate – or not made at all. "Concrete" meant that it should be an initiative for peace. "The Church must here and now be able concretely to speak the word of God, the word of power, from its own knowledge of the matter; if it does not, it is saying something different and human, a word of impotence. The Church must not proclaim principles that are always true, but only commandments that are true today. For what is 'always' true is not true 'today'. To us God is 'always' God 'today',", he said in his speech at a youth conference on peace at Ciernohorské Kúpele in the Carpathians.[29]

His work with the youth secretariat led Bonhoeffer to the other great ecumenical associations, from which the World Council of Churches was formed in 1948. In the thirties, however, these groups reacted variously to the burning issues which came out of Germany. Bonhoeffer's life cannot be understood properly without an understanding of his involvement in these various reactions. In 1931–32 the youth work of the World Alliance was united with

Free time in Prebelow. Bonhoeffer with his Berlin students, 1932. Second from left: Albrecht Schönher, later a bishop in the DDR

that of Life and Work, the movement founded in Stockholm in 1925, in which the churches as such were more strongly represented, in contrast to the World Alliance. Here for the first time Bonhoeffer met George Bell, Bishop of Chichester, who was at that time President of Life and Work, and with whom he was to form increasingly important ties of friendship. The German name for Life and Work was the Ecumenical Council for Practical Christianity. The third main association, Faith and Order, which sought to attract the theological élite, was, curiously enough, one in which Bonhoeffer never really took part. He was not attracted by the non-binding forum discussions and preferred the concrete work for peace undertaken by the World Alliance. In fact later, in the church struggle, it turned out that both the World Alliance and Life and Work supported the Confessing Church, the church opposition in Hitler's state, while Faith and Order became rather the starting-point and base for the Reich Church government which favoured Hitler.

*

Bonhoeffer started teaching and lecturing at the university in Berlin in the winter semester of 1931–32. The theological faculty had a record number of over one thousand students. Nevertheless a non-examining lecturer had to prove himself if he was to keep his audience. Bonhoeffer's lecture rooms and seminars, however, did fill.

In 1931 he began to define his position with a lecture on "The Theology of the 19th and 20th centuries". This created a stir of interest. During 1932 he dealt with the problem of the Church; twenty-five years after Harnack's famous lecture on "The Essence of Christianity" he advertised polemically in the same place his "Essence of the Church". In 1933 he applied himself to, as he said, the most difficult subject of all: christology. Then he went to London. In 1935 he tried to lecture again, travelling each week from the preachers' seminary to Berlin, on his new theme, the cost of discipleship.

His path then appears to lead from a present factual description of contemporary theology to its central core, christology. If he had been asked at the time Bonhoeffer would doubtless have replied that only this central theme was, in reality, the truly "factual" one.

Clearly Dietrich Bonhoeffer came across needs which were not really satisfied within this distinguished faculty. He satisfied them with an extraordinary personal commitment. He surprised his audience with prayers in the lecture room. He confronted them with the subject of peace, which had a shocking effect on the mass of theological students, who were already overwhelmingly Nazi sympathizers. At that time it was highly unusual, either in the Church or in the faculty, to hear such words as: "We shall not shrink here from the word 'pacificism', *the next war must be outlawed* not by elevating one commandment (as the fanatics do) above the others – the fifth, for instance – but by our

In front of the weekend hut in Biesenthal by Berlin, 1932

obedience to a commandment of God that is aimed at us today, namely that there shall be no more war because it blinds men to revelation."[30] In the Berlin lecture theatres he alone pleaded the cause of Barth's so-called dialectical theology against the great Berlin tradition running from Schleiermacher to Harnack. "My theological origin is gradually becoming suspect," he wrote to his friend Sutz, "and there is a feeling that they have nurtured a viper in their bosoms."[31]

It was not, however, simply Barth's theology which he

General Superintendent Dr Otto Dibelius

taught. It was rather an almost anti-Calvinistic theology, orientated towards Luther, which incorporated ideas from the Sermon on the Mount and the concept of discipleship, neither of which were typical of Barth at the time – in some ways, then, a theology which was critical of Barth too.

At this period a close circle of loyal theological students gathered around him. He used to spend weekends with them at a country youth hostel, and later in the hut he had

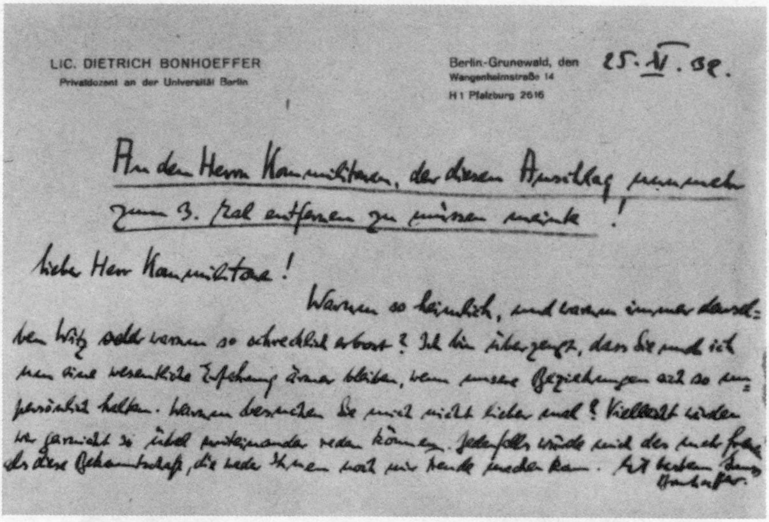

LIC. DIETRICH BONHOEFFER
Privatdozent an der Universität Berlin

Berlin-Grunewald, den 25. VI. 32.
Wangenheimstraße 14
H1 Pfalzburg 2616

An den Herrn Kommilitonen, der diesen Anschlag nunmehr zum 3. Mal entfernen zu müssen meinte!

Lieber Herr Kommilitone!

Warum so heimlich, und warum immer denselben Witz [illegible] warum so schrecklich [illegible]? Ich bin überzeugt, dass Sie und ich uns eine wesentliche Erfahrung ärmer bleiben, wenn unsere Beziehungen sich so unpersönlich halten. Warum besuchen Sie mich nicht lieber mal? Vielleicht würden wir garnicht so übel miteinander reden können. Jedenfalls würde mich das mehr freuen als diese Bekanntschaft, die [illegible] Ihnen [illegible] machen kann. Mit besten Grüssen Bonhoeffer.

For the notice-board of the student pastors at the Technical High School, Berlin–Charlottenburg, 1932

built himself at Biesenthal on the outskirts of Berlin, where they held discussions and spiritual meditations as well. With their support in 1933 he entered into the first struggle between different factions at the university; and from their number were recruited the ecumenical delegations which at times came near to acting as pressure groups.

*

The Berlin–Brandenburg Church designated Bonhoeffer for a mission which was quite new at that time: to set up and take charge of a chaplaincy for students at the Technical University in Charlottenburg. It was, in spite of all his efforts, the least successful undertaking of his life. Otto Dibelius, at that time General Superintendent of Brandenburg, had selected him for the post. There was as yet no student congregation, nor was the time ripe for one in the scientific and technical environment of such a university.

When Bonhoeffer's notices were torn down, he made a new placard: "To the fellow-student who thought he would have to take down this placard for the third time! Dear fellow-student, Why act so secretly? Why always the same joke? Or why are you so very annoyed? I am convinced that you and I are the poorer and are missing an important experience if our relationship continues to be so impersonal. Why not come and see me instead? Perhaps we would not find talking to one another so difficult. At any rate it would please me more than our present acquaintance, which can give neither of us very much pleasure. Sincerely yours, Bonhoeffer."[32]

The appointment at the Technical University ended in 1933, and the experiment was not continued.

A second task set him by the Church was to take over the instruction of an unruly confirmation class in Wedding, a working-class area of Berlin. Sometimes he would drop lectures and seminars if the children needed him, and in winter of 1931–32 he rented a room with a master baker

In the Harz Mountains with confirmation students from Wedding, 1932

in the Oderberger Strasse. He described the experience in a letter: "This is about the most outrageous district in Berlin, with the most difficult social and political conditions. At first the boys behaved as if they were crazy, so that for the first time I had real difficulties over discipline. Only one thing was any use: I simply told them stories from the Bible wholesale, in particular the eschatological passages. I also had to fall back on telling them stories about negroes. Now there is absolute quiet, the boys see to that themselves ... It is quite new to them to have to do anything other than learn the catechism."[33] He played chess with the boys, taught them English, parcelled them up each a present at Christmas, bought them material for new suits for their confirmation, took them to his hut at Biesenthal and to his parents' country house in the Harz mountains. Confirmation day was also election day, 13 March 1932; the first time Hitler stood for the Reich presidency against Hindenberg; in this area people voted for Thälmann, the communist candidate.

As a result of his experiences at Wedding, Bonhoeffer twice tried to obtain a pastorate in east Berlin. Once the parish council did not choose him, and the other time his attempt was frustrated because of his refusal to accept the Aryan clause. His experience at Wedding also inspired his decision to set up a youth club in Charlottenburg at the end of 1932, which aimed to provide unemployed youngsters with some occupation and a feeling of belonging to the community. But the events of 1933, with the witch-hunt against communists, caused the early collapse of the experiment.

Bonhoeffer's preaching services during these years became the meeting place for those who felt that in them they were hearing something essential and, at the same time, relevant. They passed on the news to their friends. "It is not our irreligiousness that is disobedience to God, but the fact that we are very glad to be religious ... very relieved when some government proclaims the Christian attitude to life ... so that the more pious we are, the less

Adolf Hitler

we have to tell ourselves that God is dangerous, that God
is not mocked." Thus ran his sermon in the Kaiser Wilhelm Memorial Church in the summer of 1932, when
Papen had become Reich Chancellor. And on Reformation Day he said: "The church that is celebrating the Reformation does not allow Luther to lie in peace, he has to
be dragged in to justify all the evil that is taking place in
the Church. The dead man is stood up in our churches,
made to stretch out his hands and point to this church,
and repeat with pathetic self-confident pathos: Here I
stand, I can do no other ... It is simply untrue, or it is
unpardonable frivolity and pride, when we take refuge
behind those words. We can do otherwise!"[34]

*

Hitler came to power on 30 January 1933. What this event would demand of Bonhoeffer was clear to him by 1934 at the latest. In a sermon in 1932 he seemed already to have a premonition: "We should not be surprised if the time comes for our church too, when the blood of martyrs will be called for. But this blood, if we really have the courage and the faithfulness to shed it, will not be so innocent and shining as that of the first witnesses. On our blood would lie our great guilt: the guilt of the useless servant."[35]

Because of his friendship with his fellow minister Franz Hildebrandt, who was "half-Jewish", and because of the Jewish connections of his twin sister's husband, Gerhard Leibholz, the consequences of ecclesiastical and political legislation by the National Socialists all too rapidly became a reality. It could only give him the determination to fight against something he had already recognized close at hand for what it was.

However, these confrontations were preceded by the real, inner decisions. They cannot be assigned dates, as sudden, separate, distinct turning-points, but they can be traced as progressive stages from the time he entered professional life in 1931. Theologically he began to study the Sermon on the Mount. Ethically he reflected on pacifism. Personally he began to practise a disciplined *praxis pietatis*. He went regularly to church (in New York Paul Lehmann had noted that this Barthian was by no means punctilious in this respect). And he meditated daily on a passage from Scripture, without any exegetical purpose at all.

Bonhoeffer practically never referred to any sudden decision about such commitment, which underlines its seriousness. Indeed in 1944, in one of his last letters from Tegel, he denies that there have been breaks in his life: "I do not think I have ever changed very much, except perhaps at the time of my first impressions abroad and under the first conscious influence of Father's personality. It was then that I turned from phraseology to reality . . . Neither of us has really had a break in our lives. Of course, we have consciously and on our own initiative broken with a good deal . . . Earlier on I sometimes longed for such a break, but today I feel differently about it."[36]

Nevertheless, he does write "longed for a break". A letter written in 1936 to a girl he knew refers to this period of his life: "I threw myself into work in a very unchristian way. An . . . ambition that many people have noticed in me, made my life difficult. . . Then something happened, something that has changed and transformed my life right up to the present day. I discovered the Bible for the first time. . . I had often preached, I had already seen a great deal of the Church, I had talked and preached about it – and yet I was still not a Christian. . . I know that at that time I turned the doctrine of Jesus Christ into something of personal advantage to myself. . . It is from this that the Bible, and especially the Sermon on the Mount, set me free. Since then everything has altered. . . It was a great liberation. It became clear to me then that the life of a servant of Jesus Christ should belong to the Church, and gradually it became clear to me how far that had to be so. Then came the 1933 crisis, which strengthened me in my conviction. . . Now my concern was the renewal of the Church and the ministry. . . . Suddenly the Christian pacifism, which I had opposed passionately only a short time before, seemed to me self-evident. And so it went on, step by step. I no longer saw or thought anything else."[37]

As has already been mentioned, Bonhoeffer had not developed the consciousness of sin that a pietistic upbringing usually inculcates. On the contrary, his upbringing had had the effect of making his superior physical, intellectual and social abilities function smoothly and automatically – at times this brought him close to despising other people. From his knowledge of himself came his understanding of the central doctrines of the Reformation of *superbia* and *cor incurvatum in se*, that heart which can neither give itself up nor accept itself. From this he developed at this period the piety and theology of a total self-dedication to Jesus. Jesus was for him the powerful master and lord, and to follow him was to gain fulfilment and a guarantee of understanding others. The Church was guided and judged by its discipleship. So his theology at this period became concentrated with increasing emphasis on the person of Christ and became more and more christocentric.

In the coming years, when Christians and ministers alike were faced with an unprecedented challenge, this total concentration on Christ in no way represented a barrier to or diminution of the reality of contemporary life. On the contrary, it created an immunization against the deceptions of National Socialism and its servants within the contemporary Church.

5 *Ministry*

Hitler's seizure of power threw Bonhoeffer into the day-to-day struggle of his church as never before. Soon he was in the forefront of the opposition, persuading and criticizing. Often his proposals for action did not command a majority among his fellow pastors. Who was this unknown twenty-seven-year-old to put himself up against those with years of experience in office?

Old friendships collapsed. Theodor Heckel, a good Lutheran theologian and earlier a valued colleague, became an official of External Affairs in the church federation office and was in charge of ecumenical questions. He was later Bonhoeffer's superior, when he was in London. As a result of his collaboration, which kept him in office until 1945, he became instead a bitterly fought opponent. New friendships arose with men working in the Church such as Martin Niemöller, who came from a totally different background, having been a captain in the First World War, and for long a declared Nationalist.

The entire Bonhoeffer family rejected Hitler from the first; there was soon acute uneasiness because Karl Bonhoeffer, as a psychiatric specialist, and Dietrich's brother-in-law, Hans von Dohnanyi, as an observer for the Minister of Justice, were drawn into the Reichstag fire investigations and the trial of van der Lubbe. His father, his brother Karl-Friedrich, his brothers-in-law Gerhard Leibholz and Walter Dress and Dietrich himself were also all affected as university teachers by the measures of the new Minister for Cultural Affairs, Bernhard Rust, and the demonstrations of the S.A. (the book-burning) in front of the university. In addition, Karl Bonhoeffer, as a specialist before the courts, was also faced with the new law hastily passed by the National Socialists and intended to suppress the transmission of hereditary diseases.

Martin Niemöller

Only two days after the seizure of power Dietrich Bonhoeffer found himself in full confrontation when, for the first and last time in his life, he was commissioned by the Berlin Broadcasting Company to give a talk over the air on the concept of the leader.[38] In it he said: "If the leader allows himself to be persuaded by those he leads who want to turn him into their idol – and those who are led will always hope for this – then the image of the leader will degenerate into that of the 'misleader'. The leader who makes an idol of himself and his office makes a mockery of

God."[39] There are only a few personal statements from Bonhoeffer during the first months of the Hitler period, and the reason is given in a letter he wrote to Erwin Sutz on 14 April 1933: "The fact that I no longer write about conditions today is because, as you know, letters cannot be regarded as private at the present time."[40] On 5 March, when the last genuine election took place, although a Protestant minister he voted for the Centre Party, in the hope that this Catholic party with its international connections might be proof against the chaos of Hitler's "legal revolution".

*

There is no official record of the reactions of the Evangelical Church to the first decisive laws passed by Hitler in March 1933. These laws demolished democracy: the Reich President's Edict for the Protection of People and State, which was in force from 28 February 1933 to 8 May 1945, provided the pretext for the measures against the churches and later against Bonhoeffer's preachers' seminary; brought the concentration camps into existence; abrogated the right to free expression of opinion, press freedom, right of assembly and privacy of the postal service; and legalized house searches and confiscations. The "Treachery Law" placed opposition to government and party on a par with betrayal of country; the "Enabling Act" dissolved the control of Parliament and the constitution; the non-Aryan law, under the extenuating name of "Decree for the Reconstruction of the Professional Civil Service", started the legal declassification of one group in the country according to race. What has been recorded for posterity are cheerful agreements from church circles to the abolition of the Weimar Republic. General Superintendents and church notables gave radio talks aimed at listeners abroad, in which they repudiated "horrible lies" and sought approval for the dawn of a peaceful and legal revolution to stem the advance of Bolshevism.

In the meantime Dietrich Bonhoeffer devised plans with

his American friend Paul Lehmann, who was then in Berlin, as to how best to keep the Chief Rabbi in New York informed about the first major Jewish boycott. When the non-Aryan law of 7 April 1933 first excluded Jews from the Civil Service Bonhoeffer, as one of the first churchmen, drew up a paper with six theses on the subject, "The Church and the question of the Jews". When he gave the paper at an April meeting of ministers, some left the gathering in protest. None the less, he was still able to have the lecture printed in June 1933.[41]

The paper shows a Bonhoeffer who in 1933 was still doing everything he could not to argue from a democratic-humanitarian angle. As a good Lutheran he acknowledged the State's right to settle even the Jewish question legitimately. This was nothing new for his audience and counted as good theology at the time. But then he demanded – and this was considered bad theology – that within this framework the Church must, firstly, ask the State "whether it could answer for its action as legitimate political action. . . . Today the Church must ask this question as regards the Jewish problem with the utmost clarity; secondly, the Church has an unconditional obligation to the victims of any social order, regardless of whether they belong to the Christian community or not; thirdly, when the Church sees the state exercising too little or too much law and order, it is its task not simply to bind the wounds of the victims beneath the wheel, but also to put a spoke in the wheel itself."[42] It was for the time a very courageous statement.

So Bonhoeffer discussed first and foremost not just the question of the church membership of Jews – although he did this too – but their basic human rights in the German State. Later the Confessing Church was to consider the Aryan clause almost exclusively as it affected the Church and not the State. This seemed a great deal at the time, although in retrospect it was, of course, far too little.

At that time Bonhoeffer did not intend that the recognition of the third possibility in his paper, that of the political opposition merely hinted at here, should be left to the decision of the individual; it was to be carried out and authorized by an "Evangelical Council". In placing his hopes here on the ecumenical movement he over-estimated its capabilities and was soon to be disappointed. And years later he eventually decided, without any corporate help from Church or Council, on his own responsibility to put a spoke in the wheel himself.

*

In summer 1933 events overtook the ecclesiastical sector. Bonhoeffer was constantly involved in trying to change reaction into action.

The National Socialists in the Church, the "German Christians" as they called themselves, had been trying to gain power since April. In June the General Superintendents in Prussia were removed and a State Commissar (August Jäger) appointed. Hitler made Ludwig Müller, a chaplain to the forces, his confidential adviser on church matters, and the German Christians nominated him as their candidate for Reich Bishop. Bonhoeffer and his students duplicated resolutions, he spoke against Müller at protest meetings and conferred with Gerhard Jacobi, minister at the Kaiser Wilhelm Memorial Church, and Niemöller, who now moved into the centre of the opposition in Berlin. Bonhoeffer suggested that the ministers should embark upon a strike of funeral services, that is, revive the ancient measure of an interdict, for as long as the State Commissar was in control. No one considered this feasible – even though later, in 1941, the Norwegian Church used it with success in its own struggle. On 23 July 1933 the German Christians won the recently instituted church elections by a large majority. Because of disagreements about the conduct of the election, Bonhoeffer went, with Jacobi, to Gestapo headquarters for the first time. He suggested to his fellow-ministers, again without awakening any response, that they should leave a church which he saw becoming heretical.

Reich Bishop Ludwig Müller, commonly known as "Reibi"

Defeat in the elections changed the emphasis of the opposition's struggle. Their aim now was to make the winners of the key positions in the Church consider the question of what their confession, teaching and actions should be; they wanted to question them about their confession and work out a new creed for themselves in order to combat distortions. During those weeks, in groups of ministers, all sorts of "confessions" were formulated, that is, statements which were intended to explain what the old confession of faith really meant today. These efforts were to be synthensized and formulated competently and representatively in Bethel. Professor Hermann Sasse of Erlangen and Dietrich Bonhoeffer were invited to edit a first draft and in August they produced what was later to become known as the "Bethel Confession"[43] which was, as it were, a forerunner of the famous Barmen Declaration.

Because of his lack of success at this period, Bonhoeffer considered withdrawing from the front line of the struggle: he gave a trial sermon to a German-speaking congregation in London and in fact took up his ministry there in the second half of October.

Before that, at the time of the introduction of the Aryan Clause into the Church by the "Brown" General Synod on 6 September 1933, Bonhoeffer was involved in the setting up of Niemöller's Pastors' Emergency League, for the support of fellow-ministers who were Jewish Christians. This was the organization which took the place of the former opposition group, the Young Reformers' Movement, which was now crumbling and which anticipated the formation of the "Confessing Church" at the Barmen Synod in May 1934. Bonhoeffer formulated the first draft of the statement of personal commitment, together with Niemöller. After that he left for an ecumenical conference in the Balkans to inform leading ecumenists on the background to events. At the National Synod in Wittenberg on 27 September, when Ludwig Müller was made Reich Bishop, he and his friends pinned their leaflets on trees and fences.

*

When he arrived in London he wrote a long letter to Barth (24 October 1933): "I am at last writing you the letter that I meant to send you six weeks ago and that would perhaps have resulted in a totally different turn in my personal life ... I have now 'freely' decided, without feeling that I am free as far as you are concerned. I wanted to ask you whether I ought to go to London parish or not. I would simply have believed that you would tell me the right thing. ... The London offer was made to me in July. ... At the same time I was offered a parish in the east, there was no doubt about my choice. Then came the Aryan clause in Prussia and I knew that I could not take the parish I had longed for in this very district, unless I wanted to give up my total opposition to this church,

The manse in London, in which Bonhoeffer lived 1933–35

unless I wanted to lose all credibility in the eyes of my congregation right from the start, and unless I wanted to abandon my solidarity with the Jewish Christian ministers – my best friend is one and is faced at the moment with nothing; he is coming to me in England now. So there remained the alternative of being a university lecturer or a minister, although not a minister in Prussia. . . . I felt that I was in conflict quite radically with all my friends and I did not understand why. I felt more and more isolated from them by my views, although I still had, and kept, a close personal relationship with them – and all this made me worried and unsure of myself, and I was fearful of being led astray by dogmatism – and I saw no real reason why I should be able to understand things better or be more right than so many good and able pastors whom I respect – so I thought it was perhaps time to go into the wilderness for a while and simply do parish work as un-obtrusively as possible. The danger of making a gesture seemed to me greater at the moment than that of retreating into silence. This is how it happened. . . . Now you will soon be in Berlin and I cannot be there. I feel too that I

have been disloyal to you personally through my departure. You will perhaps not be able to understand this, but
it is very real to me. Yet in spite of everything I am eternally happy to be in a parish and so quite away from it all.
And then I hope too that here the ecumenical problems
will become clearer. For that is work I intend to continue
here. Perhaps the German Church can be given some encouragement in this way. . . ."

Karl Barth wrote a lively if severe reply to this letter. He
said that Bonhoeffer should in no circumstances now play
Elijah under the juniper tree or Jonah under the gourd.
"You ought to drop all these intellectual frills and special
pleadings, however interesting, and concentrate on one
thing alone, that you are a German and that your
Church's house is on fire, that you know enough and also
know how to say it well enough, to be capable of bringing
help, and that fundamentally you ought to return to your
post by the next ship! Or let us say, the ship after next."[44]

Bonhoeffer's church at Sydenham, London, 1934

Bonhoeffer showed the reply to his father, who commented: "It is indeed a fine testimony of a fiery spirit. I should not like to comment on the point at issue. I think, however, that there is value in seeing things from a distance and bringing influence to bear from outside and above all in saving one's energy for the right moment."[45]

For a year and a half Bonhoeffer was pastor to two very small parishes in London: the German Evangelical Congregation in Sydenham (founded in 1875 by well-to-do-German businessmen) and the much older German Reformed Congregation of St Paul in the East End, composed mainly of German tradesmen. As an attempt at evading the issue by quiet pastoral work, the interlude was a complete failure. He wrote to his brother Karl-Friedrich in January 1934: ". . . here you find yourself too close at hand not to want to take part in everything and yet too far away really to join actively in anything. I have found this very difficult in the last few weeks."[46] Protest letters were sent off, envoys arrived from Berlin. The authorities at home were worried because the Archbishop of Canterbury asked Bonhoeffer to come to Lambeth Palace to give him a report, and because their colleagues in England made representations to the President of the Reich. Bonhoeffer was in Berlin every few weeks.

Even though every free minute was devoted to the Church struggle and to ecumenical affairs, Bonhoeffer carried out the pastoral care of his parishes devotedly. He appealed to church elders and members for help for emigrés from Germany, political or Jewish refugees, such as Gottfried Treviranus or Arnim T. Wegner. There was no question but that he should also involve his congregation in the struggle for the recognition of the Confessing Church; eventually the leaders broke away from the Church External Affairs Office in Berlin, of which Heckel was in charge.

*

In Germany Bonhoeffer's friends were meanwhile constructing the final barrier against an amalgamation of the various Evangelical Churches. From 29 to 31 May 1934 the famous Confessing Synod took place at Barmen. One hundred and thirty-eight delegates from all the Lutheran, United and Reformed regional churches, under pressure from Berlin's new centralization measures, unanimously accepted the world-renowned six clauses against the false doctrines of the German Christians and their church government. They had been drafted by Barth. Their first repudiation clause ran: "We reject the false doctrine that the Church should acknowledge, as the source of its message over and above God's Word, any other events, powers, figures and truths as divine revelation." This renewal of the Reformation claim *solus Christus* was seen by all as directed at Hitler's claims of 1933.

Dietrich Bonhoeffer was not at Barmen. For him, however, these six theses meant the fulfilment of everything for which he had fought for so long and which he had thought no longer possible. This was the real moment of birth for the Confessing Church. Now he wanted to see results immediately: the organization of Councils of Brethren and their recognition as emergency governments of the Church at all levels.

The feat of unanimity at Barmen had been achieved mainly by Hans Asmussen's introductory address presenting the six theses, which had carried the synod with it. In those days Asmussen was one of the greatest protagonists in the Confessing Church. But with this interpretation he gave the Confessing Church, at the moment of its inception, something that, although at first scarcely recognized, was one day to force men like Bonhoeffer to ask new questions and to make their own decisions, which were then passed over in silence by the Confessing Church. Asmussen had made the six theses acceptable to all those at the synod by explicitly deleting any political dimension from their protest, and instead linking the protest with the critical detachment from the Enlightenment and the nineteenth century – and the National Socialists of course rejected the

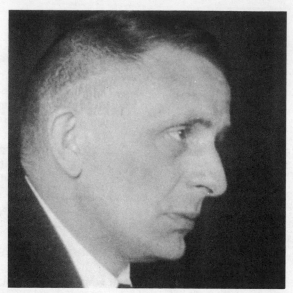

Hans Asmussen

Enlightenment too. He said: "If we protest against them [the claims of 1933 which were intended to restrict the Church], we do so not as members of the nation against the most recent episode in our nation's history, nor as citizens against the state, nor as subjects against those in authority" (this was said a few weeks before the Röhm *putsch* and the assassination of Dollfuss); then he continued, we protest against the phenomenon "which has been slowly preparing the devastation of the Church for more than 200 years", and which "set up reason, culture, aesthetic feeling and progress . . . as binding claims on the Church".[47] In saying this Asmussen expressed what many at Barmen were thinking.

Barth and Bonhoeffer both dissociated themselves, at first unobtrusively, but later more and more emphatically, from the apolitical viewpoint described above, which was that of the Confessing Church too. So it is understandable how Bonhoeffer eventually later saw himself forced alone

into involvement in the conspiracy. As far as the linking of
1933 with the revolution of 1789 and the progress of the
Enlightenment is concerned – a very welcome reference at
the time – it explains how Bonhoeffer could one day (in
fact, in 1944 in Tegel) find he wanted to work out anew
the relationship of the Christian faith to the Enlightenment and to emancipation, in fact, its relationship to a
world come of age.

*

At the time, however, Bonhoeffer was fairly unaffected by
these two aspects of the Barmen Synod expressed by
Asmussen. He was simply pleased about the six theses and
wanted to encourage respect for the Barmen decision.
From his standpoint this meant persuading the ecumenical
movement to recognize the Confessing Synod and in practice to keep its distance from the Berlin church government. Should the ecumenical leaders still invite Heckel and
the External Affairs Office to their conferences? Should
Bonhoeffer appear at these conferences in company with
Heckel's supporters? These were the questions facing him.
    He had already written to Henriod, the General Sec-
retary of Life and Work in Geneva, shortly before the
Barmen Synod. "My dear Henriod, . . . I would have liked
to discuss the situation with you again, since I am gradually coming to consider the slowness of ecumenical pro-
cedure as irresponsible. A decision has to be taken in the
end and we cannot go on waiting for a sign from heaven
that will suddenly drop the solution to the problem into
our lap. Even the ecumenical movement has to make up its
mind and is subject to error, a general human fate. But not
to act and not to take a stand, simply for fear of making a
mistake when others – I mean our brethren in Germany –
have to make infinitely difficult decisions every day, seems
to me to be almost a contradiction of love. . . . 'Allow me
to go before. . . .' says the Gospel – how often we use it as
a pretext, and yet here it really is now or never, 'Too late'
means 'Never'. If the ecumenical movement does not see

this now and if there are none who are 'violent to take heaven by force' (Matthew 11:12), then the ecumenical movement is no longer the Church, but a useless association for making fine speeches . . .

"I am writing to you like this because I felt your last letter to me had similar overtones. And if all the 'wise', the old and influential here, are unwilling to join us and hold back out of all sorts of misgivings – then go forward yourself, attack, do not let yourself be stopped or misled . . ."[48]

In this struggle George Bell, Bishop of Chichester, and at that time President of the Ecumenical Council for Life and Work, became an advocate of the Confessing Church. Bonhoeffer kept him in constant touch with the latest information from Berlin. He advised the Bishop on a pastoral letter and wrote to him: the moment has come "to take a definite stand either in the form of an ultimatum or in a public expression of sympathy for the Opposition pastors . . . so please send a letter to all the ecumenical churches and warn them."[49] On the Bishop's recommendation the Ecumenical Conference at Fanö in August 1934 chose the head of the Confessing Synod, Präses Karl Koch, and Bonhoeffer, as members of the Ecumenical Council.

Bonhoeffer did not, however, achieve what he wanted: the exclusion of the Reich Government Church. The loose associations, bound by their statutes, could not manage to make such a decision. Bonhoeffer himself always acted as if the inner logic of the Barmen decision were already an external fact – not because he was blind to realities, but because he wanted to consolidate elements ready for development. He acted similarly, for instance, in selecting the Youth Delegation from Germany, for which he was responsible. His strict insistence on people who approved the Barmen decision led to conflicts. For this reason in 1937 Bonhoeffer gave up his official ecumenical post.

To his friends in Geneva he seemed obstinate in the extreme. In reality he was committed totally to finding the right time and place for the voice of peace to be heard, a

With Jean Lasserre (France). Ecumenical Conference at Fanö,
August 1934

peace which it was forbidden even to mention in Germany. In Fanö in 1934 the fervour of his peace sermon had made a profound impression when he addressed the wavering assembly on the justification for its existence. "As a branch of ecumenism, the World Council ... has heard God's call to peace and directs his command to the peoples of the world. Our theological task here therefore consists solely in hearing this commandment as a binding commandment and not discussing it as an open question ... Who gives the call to peace so that the world hears it, so that the world is forced to hear it? So that all nations have to rejoice? The individual Christian cannot do it. ... Only the one great ecumenical Council of Christ's Holy Church throughout the world can proclaim it, so that the world, gnashing its teeth, has to hear the word of peace and so that the nations rejoice because this Church of Christ takes the weapons out of its sons' hands in the name of Christ, and forbids the war and shouts out the peace of Christ over the raging world... The hour is at hand – the world bristles with weapons ... the fanfares of war could be sounded tomorrow – why are we still waiting? Do we ourselves want to be guilty too, guilty as never before?"[50]

*

Dietrich Bonhoeffer's actions in these months were without doubt centred on the Church and the ecumenical movement. None the less the dividing wall between this and the political dimension of the time had become very thin. There was no censorship on letters that Bonhoeffer, while in London, sent to Erwin Sutz in Switzerland. He wrote to him in 1934: " .... although I work in the Church opposition with all my energies, it is quite clear to me that such opposition is only an interim transitional stage to a quite different opposition, and that the men of this first preliminary skirmish are in a small way the men of that second struggle. And I believe that all Christendom must pray with us that 'resistance unto death' will come and that men will be found who will suffer it (28 April 1934). I consider any discussion between Hitler and Barth would be completely pointless and even no longer admissible. Hitler has shown himself very clearly for what he is and the Church ought to realize with whom it has to reckon. Isaiah, after all, did not go to Sennacherib. We have tried often enough – too often – to make Hitler understand what we mean. Perhaps we have never done it in the right way, but then Barth will not do it in the right way either. Hitler cannot and must not hear. So it is the other way round: he is obdurate and so forces us to be hearers instead. The Oxford Group (Frank Buchmann) was naïve enough to try to convert Hitler – a ludicrous misconception of what is happening. We have to be converted, not Hitler. . . ."[51]

Thoughts of anything like a political conspiracy in which he himself would be involved did not arise until years later. For the present Bonhoeffer again took up his plans of going to India. This time, through Bell and Niebuhr, he managed to obtain a personal invitation from Gandhi, the greatest thinker and activist of non-violent

German youth delegation at the Ecumenical Youth Conference, Fanö, August 1934

resistance, which he wanted to study in its original home and form. Perhaps here was an opportunity to discover how a follower of Christ, a Christian pastor, could offer appropriate resistance without repudiating political responsibility.

Once again the projected journey to India came to nothing, for Bonhoeffer was called upon to return home and to work in the Confessing Church for the "renewal of the pastorate".

6 *Preachers' Seminary*

During the next five years, Bonhoeffer's work in one of the Confessing Church's seminaries for preachers brought him a time of fulfilment such as he had never before experienced. It was, however, also a time when he was deeply concerned about the disintegration of church opposition to Hitler.

In the Evangelical Church a preachers' seminary was the ecclesiastical institute which candidates for the second examination and for ordination had to attend for a few months, after their studies at state university faculties and their first examination. In his own case in 1928–29 Bonhoeffer had done everything he could to avoid such an institution – poorly equipped in comparison with a faculty – and its pressures. He had considered it a pure waste of time, which he was able to escape because of his habilitation thesis. Now he was to be head of just such an institute. However, this preachers' seminary had come into existence as a result of the Barmen Synod, that is, it had been founded by the now active Emergency Church Government of the Confessing Synod and its Council of Brethren, which was regarded as illegal by the Reich church government. After the first summer Bonhoeffer could write: "The summer of 1935 has been the most fulfilled time of my life, both in terms of relationships with others and of my profession."[52]

*

The Confessing Church's seminaries were opened with great zeal in 1935. Reich Bishop Ludwig Müller's attacks on the regional churches were verging on fiasco by the end of 1934. The growth of the Confessing Church's Emergency Groups reached a high point at this time. Now the ordinands, ready to serve the Church, were merely waiting

77

Winter 1934–35

to be put to use. So admission to a newly-established seminary, instead of the unpopular alternative of entry to an official institute, became an eagerly awaited eventuality for the ordinands. Any arrangement, however provisional, was welcome. To beg for beds, bread and books was merely a prelude to the longed-for beginning. Bonhoeffer himself had his extensive library and his Bechstein piano brought to Pomerania when they moved into the house at Finkenwalde near Stettin. He had them installed not in his own modest room, but in the common living-room where they could be used by everyone.

The first chilly weeks of May, however, had to be spent in a sort of youth hostel, behind the Baltic dunes of Zingst. None the less, fascination with the novelty of it made all the ordinands forget the lack of amenities. The young director read out to them something they had never heard before: the chapters about *cheap grace*, by which the Protestant churches had poisoned themselves, and *costly grace*, which can be experienced only in discipleship and handed on; in fact, chapters of the book which was soon to make Bonhoeffer known in church circles. Eberhard Bethge, later Bonhoeffer's friend, was among those present at these first readings.

It soon became evident, however, that the listeners were not so completely in harmony with their teacher as they had at first believed. At Tempelhof on 1 May 1935 Hitler announced the new law on military service. The ordinands listening around the wireless in Zingst were delighted to be able at last to prove their often suspect patriotism by doing military service. They were somewhat taken aback to notice that the head of their institute did not share their enthusiasm. He seemed to regard the new law as a misfortune in general and for himself in particular. He pointed

The garden side of the *Gutshaus*, to which the Preachers' Seminary moved. Finkenwalde by Stettin, 1935

out that for Christians there was the possibility of refusing to undertake military service. But at the time this was an idea far removed from the minds of ordinands in the Confessing Church or their Councils of Brethren. It was simply not envisaged either in the teaching or the practice of the Lutheran tradition in Germany. The decreasing number of Christians who entertained such ideas were regarded as sectarians or outsiders. Catastrophe had to come before that would change: the majority of those sitting there listening in some bewilderment were to die on the French and Russian fronts, although they had imagined a very different objective in life; and the man who questioned them so disturbingly was to die as a political conspirator, although he too at the time viewed his future contribution very differently.

At the time the listeners were scarcely conscious of that juxtaposition. At first their questions were merely theoretical: should "discipleship" be practised in this way? Should

With Eberhard Bethge on the joint pastorate at Gross-Schlönwitz, Further Pomerania

Ecumenical Conference in Chamby, August 1936. George Bell, Bishop of Chichester, tries to explain. Left to right: Wilhelm Zoellner, Chairman of the Reich Church Office; Karl Koch, President of the Confessing Church; Bell; Otto Dibelius.

the threatening dangers which grew out of the church struggle be fanned yet further by such pacificist ideas? These dangers would soon reach Finkenwalde. On this point, at least, they were all united.

*

In the summer of 1935 Hitler set up a Church Ministry. The new Minister of Church Affairs, Hans Kerrl, gave the highly respected General Superintendent Wilhelm Zoellner the task of "pacifying" the Church with so-called Church Committees. These Committees were to be composed of representatives of the Confessing Church, the

81

German Christians and the neutrals. Zoellner's call for co-operation included the oath: "We affirm the National Socialist development of our nation on the basis of race, blood and land." Should they co-operate or not? A profound rift appeared in the ranks of the Confessing Church. There was a tempting proposal to continue merely as a Confessing Movement, but no longer as a Confessing Church with its own Emergency Church Government. Previously it had been a question of refusing to obey the heretical laws of the Church – many people found this possible; now it was a question of direct disobedience to the laws of the state "authorities" – which frightened off many people. In any case – was not "pacification" an admirable aim? The Confessing Church diminished noticeably in size; and finally only a small group persisted in an isolated illegality. In Finkenwalde, however, the situation was not immediately apparent.

On 2 December 1935 Reich Minister Kerrl issued the decree "for the Implementation of the Law for the Protection of the Evangelical Church". It declared illegal all "powers of ecclesiastical government or administration vested in groups or associations within the Church". Thus the running of a preachers' seminary under the Council of Brethren was illegal. The new situation, in all its severity, was immediately plain to Bonhoeffer. That same evening of 2 December he called all the ordinands together and in view of the new situation released them from any obligation to remain. They all stayed. There were initially no repercussions for the seminary, existing as it did in its remote corner. Two years were to elapse before the Gestapo appeared and closed down the house.

Even then Bonhoeffer found a way of working with ordinands of the Confessing Church for another two and a half years, in the "collective pastorates". It was customary to assign ordinands to pastorates with parish ministers and this was not contested by the official church, so Bonhoeffer searched out ministers who were prepared to take curates of the Confessing Church. During the week they were

Reich Minister Hans Kerrl

to meet together in an empty vicarage and continue their studies with Bonhoeffer. In the nearby districts of Köslin and Schlawe suitable pastors were found. Everything was arranged discreetly by the two excellent superintendents Block and Onnasch. Bonhoeffer now went for half of each week to teach in Köslin and the other half in Gross-Schlönwitz near Schlawe, and after 1939 in a forest house at nearby Sigurdshof.

Since they were short of space there, some of his books and manuscripts were left in an attic at Finkenwalde and later were lost. Some were sent back to his parents' home. In 1935 they had moved to the Marienburger Allee in the West End, next door to their daughter Ursula Schleicher and her family. Since Bonhoeffer no longer had a permanent home after the closure of Finkenwalde, his attic room in the Marienburger Allee became increasingly important to him, and was later a place for discussions between the conspirators.

Sometimes Bonhoeffer, who wanted to write, suffered from this nomadic existence.

In March 1940 the Gestapo arrived once again and closed the house in Sigurdshof. In the meantime the ordinands had almost all gone to the trenches.

*

Bonhoeffer's seminary was similar to the parallel seminaries run by Hans Iwand in East Prussia and Gerhard Gloege in Silesia, in that its studies were principally concerned with theology, both biblical and based on the Confessional writings. Similarly they all acted as a pressure group in the decisions about the Church struggle, and all experienced the increase in arrests and the defection of some of their number seeking "legalization" for the sake of recognition by the official church leadership and the benefits of more peaceful work and a proper vicarage. What distinguished Bonhoeffer's seminary from the others was the style of its *vita communis*, which gave rise to a great deal of comment. Bonhoeffer himself practised and required of the others a daily half-hour of silence and meditation on the Scriptures. He succeeded in restoring the long-forgotten practice of personal confession. "Spiritual exercises" and meditation were, however, so unusual that there were soon accusations of "monasticism" and "legalism". In a letter to Barth on 19 September 1936 he wrote: "The reproach that it is legalistic does not hurt me. What could be legalistic about a Christian making an effort to learn what prayer is and spending a good deal of his time in learning about it? When one of the leading men in the Confessing Church said to me recently: 'We have no time for meditation now, the ordinands have to learn how to preach and catechize', it seemed to me to reveal either a total incomprehension of what a young theologian today is like or a criminal ignorance of the real roots of preaching and catechesis".[53]

Later Bonhoeffer recorded his experiences of this style of spiritual life in a community of future ministers in the

In Gross-Schlönwitz, 1938

short book *Life Together*. With the book of his letters and papers from Tegel prison, it was and still is the work which enjoyed the greatest popular success when published.

He was now, however, occupied with another problem closely related to the practice of this way of life: he could not continue from one course to the next on his own. Instead he envisaged that the new arrivals would be received into an existing circle where a communal life was already practised.

So at the end of the first course in the autumn of 1935 he asked several ordinands to stay and form a community with him, albeit in a very loose form. Surprisingly the various provincial Councils of Brethren released five ordinands, among them Eberhard Bethge, who had expressed a wish to stay. This community with *convivium*, unique in Protestant Germany at the time, called itself "The House of Brethren". There were no vows. They obeyed a discipline of prayer, shared all the financial outgoings, which were largely subsidized from Bonhoeffer's salary, undertook obligations in the teaching and life of the seminary and of the neighbouring parishes of the Confessing Church. As far as the seminary was concerned, the House of Brethren provided a strong backbone, an intensive continuum in the extensive activities of church politics, a refuge for the former students now vulnerable in their isolated parishes.

With the transition to the collective pastorate in 1937–38, the experiment of the House of Brethren came to an all too early end. In spite of its cursory nature the experiment was, nevertheless, of enormous importance. Its essence lay not simply in ensuring continuity in the preachers' seminary, with its half-yearly change of students. It also represented a contribution to the "renewal of the pastorate", with which Bonhoeffer had long been concerned. The experiment served as a practical criticism of the individual parochial ministry with all its traditional rights, burdens and weaknesses.

In his request to the Council of Brethren to inaugurate the House of Brethren in the preachers' seminary, Bonhoeffer described their aims: the content and style of pre-aching can be sustained with greater objectivity and courage in a communal life than in isolation. Proclamation, and not an introverted contemplation, remains the principal objective. The questions about Christian life which are now put with such urgency on all sides cannot be answered in the abstract, but only from a concrete life together and a common meditation on the commandments of Christ. The theological question of discipleship is thus all-important. Therefore a group of pastors who are always available, and who renounce their traditional privileges, is essential. In a brotherhood with a communal life they will find the concentration necessary for service to others outside.

This was, however, no less than a request for the approval of a new form of pastorate. The question was an acute one, because the traditional ministry in the parish had become a major source of temptation in the Church struggle. The relatively secure life in the parochial ministry, even under National Socialism, proved an attractive objective by now for many who lessened their open witness to the truth. Bonhoeffer stubbornly opposed the efforts of a few of the ordinands to "legalize" their situation. In 1939 he implored those of their number who were in favour of legalization: "Firstly, anyone who worries only about himself at this time, is deceiving himself about the community of the Church. . . Secondly, anyone who urges us to find a solution to all problems under any circumstances is giving bad counsel. . . Thirdly, anyone who tries to make us nervous and unsure of ourselves by arguing that we should at least salvage what we have got, that enough has already been snatched away from us, should be countered by the fact that we cannot expect anything from out present given situation . . . Let us not then persuade ourselves that over there in the consistorial ranks we would be free to deal with the essential items. Once there we would have surrendered all inner authority because we had not held firm to the truth."[54]

It must be admitted that after 1945 the attempts to reproduce Bonhoeffer's practice were almost total failures. The restoration of the parochial ministry was a complete success. Bonhoeffer's experiment was described as introverted contemplation, a reproach based on a misunderstanding of the issue and its function. In the Finkenwalde period it provided both vital stability for young ministers in face of the pressures to conform, and also strength to

Houses in the Marienburger Allee: No. 42 (Schleicher) and No. 43 (Bonhoeffer)

43 Marienburger Allee: Bonhoeffer with his Mother and the Schleicher children, 1939

maintain independence in their Christian life.

Bonhoeffer's work at Finkenwalde bore fruit in two books: *The Cost of Discipleship* and *Life Together*. From the day of their publication in 1937 and 1939 respectively they were read eagerly by the laity for the vital exposition they gave of what grace really is and is not. Some chapters are still felt to be vital and effective today all over the world. In addition they make an important contribution to the problem of a credible form for the ministry, which has become really urgent today. It almost seems as if the development of contemporary society contains ever more potent disintegrating elements in its conventional structure; the National Socialist enemies did not eliminate these but used them shamelessly as inducements. Bonhoeffer replied not with memoranda or debate, but with practical experiment. And this experiment cut across the old identification of the office of preacher with the office of minister and gave indisputable precedence to the former.

*

The Finkenwalde period saw violent attacks on Bonhoeffer's reputation as a theologian, and brought the first tangible harassment by the Gestapo; but it also provided many new contacts and friendships, and it marked a change in direction towards the decisive years of his life spent outside the private and inner ecclesiastical sphere.

In 1936 there was a widespread rumour that Bonhoeffer had declared that anyone without a "red card" would not go to heaven. The "red card" was the sign of a person's membership of and allegiance to the Confessing Church. Bonhoeffer had in fact joined in the controversies about Zoellner's church committees with an essay on *The Community of the Church*, and had demanded action strictly on the lines of the Barmen Declaration. This had produced a torrent of views for and against him, including even the demand that the Councils of Brethren dissociate themselves finally from this radical theologian Bonhoeffer. They did not do so. The bowdlerized sentence had run:

"Anyone who knowingly separates himself off from the Confessing Church in Germany, separates himself off from salvation."[55] His aim was to counteract the fatal individualization of salvation and to defend the place from which a voice could still be heard clearly speaking for Christ and for those who had been silenced.

The snare which was to close around Bonhoeffer's freedom now began to tighten. When in 1936 he and the seminarians returned from a trip to Denmark and Sweden, which had been widely reported in the press there, he was removed from his teaching post at the University by the Minister of Education, unless he gave up Finkenwalde. In 1937 the closure of the seminary followed. In 1938 the Gestapo forced their way into a Berlin session of those in charge of education in the Confessing Church, and served a notice of "prohibition on entry" to the capital on all non-residents, including Bonhoeffer. This threatened his communications with his parents' home, where he was able to receive news of political events behind the scenes only by word of mouth. His father succeeded, however, in having the general prohibition turned into a partial one, that is, he was allowed into Berlin to visit his parents. The prohibition on taking part in church activities in Berlin was never lifted. So everything had to take place from then on – even church matters – in the Marienburger Allee. Perhaps surprisingly, although he was working illegally as director of a seminary, Bonhoeffer continued to be spared imprisonment. Seminaries and collective pastorates were, after all, not important concerns.

His work in the seminary and the financial worries about its maintenance brought Bonhoeffer into contact with the leading figures of the Confessing Church in Pomerania. They were mainly landowners. Among them were outstanding patrons of the Church with ancient rights, who had Bonhoeffer's efforts for the renewal of the pastorate very much at heart: for instance, Reinhold von Thadden-Trieglaff, then head of the Pomeranian Confessing Synod; the Kleists, among them Hans-Jürgen von

Kleist-Retzow of Kieckow and especially his mother, Ruth von Kleist-Retzow of Klein-Krössin. The latter was a highly accomplished woman theologically. When she lived in Stettin with her school-age grandchildren, she came regularly to the seminary services at Finkenwalde. Among the children at the time was her granddaughter Maria von Wedemeyer, who was eventually to become engaged to Dietrich Bonhoeffer. At Klein-Krössin Bonhoeffer later wrote substantial sections of his *Ethics*. And there, as in the neighbouring house of Ewald von Kleist at Schmenzin, early conspiracy discussions took place, which later in Berlin were to lead to firm links with the group of conspirators. But the road there was far from rapid or straight.

7   Conspiracy

During the five years that Bonhoeffer was concerned with setting up the preachers' seminary, political development in Germany had moved at an increasingly threatening pace. The assurance given by the Church at Barmen in 1934: "We will not interfere in politics", was turned by the Nazis into a ruthless threat: "Beware of any interference in politics." On 11 September 1934 Bonhoeffer had already written to Sutz: "We can no longer continue to exercise an attitude of restraint and justify it theologically as far as the actions of the State are concerned – such discretion is nothing but fear. 'Open your mouth for the dumb!' Proverbs 31:8 – who in the Church today realizes that this is the least of the Bible's demands at such a time? And then there is the problem of military service and war, etc., etc."[56] When the Confessing Synods made courageous declarations on acts of state policy towards the Church, Bonhoeffer always immediately examined whether they had also made a statement on the Jewish question as a whole. The sum total was meagre. The restrictive formula announced by Asmussen in Barmen, *solus Christus*, Christ alone, brought about an increasingly oppressive tendency towards abstaining from political participation in face of increasing injustice. Although it was of course an enforced caution, the Church has to accept its share of guilt.

In 1938, from Switzerland, Barth expressed his anxiety over the apolitical attitude of the Councils of Brethren. With his essay *Rechtfertigung und Recht* (Justification and Justice) in which he set out the theological basis for his concern, he caused considerable hardship for his friends in Germany. Bonhoeffer felt that he was being driven ever more inexorably towards a decision. Even the bravest sermon, the theology of discipleship and the *praxis pietatis*

The Pastors' Seminar in Stockholm, March 1936

could not prevent the feeling of being forced into complicity with Hitler's policies on war and the Jews. The
Confessing Church had become a place of "Inner emigration". Ought it to be left in this state of emigration? What
should or could Bonhoeffer do in his position?

*

He was not immediately sure what he should do. At first
the year 1938 saw the conflict aggravated for him to the
point at which he tried to evade it. In 1938 his church
plumbed the depths of its weakness; painful decisions were
required of him personally; in the political field the first
attempts at conspiracy were initiated.

Ecclesiastically, the official Reich Church government
decreed, as a birthday gift for Hitler after the invasion of
Austria, that all pastors should take an oath of allegiance
to Hitler personally. Initially the Confessing pastors re-

sisted, on the grounds that the matter was already covered by their ordination vows, but then during the course of the summer almost all the pastors who had been established officially in local parishes took this oath, on the grounds that for them as for the military, an oath was not forbidden if the State required it. After the oath had been taken, Bormann announced from the Party office that neither the Party nor the State had ever placed any importance on it. It was an embarrassing announcement which caused general consternation. Since, as a Confessing pastor he was not on the official lists of the authorities, Bonhoeffer had not been asked to swear, but he had campaigned vigorously against the taking of the oath, and had described the Confessing Synod's agreement to the oath-taking as a fearful defeat.[57] He wrote: "Does the synod see how it has endangered its word through its last session?"

During the Sudeten crisis leading figures in the Confessing Synod produced a liturgy containing a confession of the Church's guilt and a prayer that the danger of war might be averted. It was denounced by the S.S. newspaper *Das Schwarze Korps* as "treasonable action in clerical garb". As a result many previously sympathetic Lutherans dissociated themselves from the authors of the liturgy. Tragically enough these same authors, and the Provisional Church Government of the Confessing Synod as well, were obliged to dissociate themselves from the Swiss Karl Barth, when in a famous letter to the Prague theologian Josef Hromadka he called upon the Czechoslovaks to offer military resistance to Hitler's regiments in Christ's name.

After the burning of the synagogues and the terrorizing and deportation of the Jews during the so-called "Crystal Night" of 9 November 1938, the Confessing Church lacked the courage for any further public statements.

Personally, Bonhoeffer was affected when in late summer came the law requiring the passports of non-Aryans to be stamped with an "I" (Israel, for men) or "S" (Sarah, for women). The family heard in advance

Burning synagogue in Berlin, 9 November 1938 (The "Crystal Night")

from Hans von Dohnanyi that this law was about to be passed, and Bonhoeffer's twin sister Sabine Leibholz and her husband Gerhard decided hastily on emigration, which they had long feared but for which they had made no serious preparations. The *Schwarze Korps* wrote of the "total annihilation" of the Jews if war broke out. In September Dietrich accompanied the family part of the way to Switzerland, from where they went to England.

The Sudeten crisis also had the effect of accelerating the process of military call-up, which was now affecting men of Bonhoeffer's age. Could Bonhoeffer burden the Confessing Church, already heavily under attack and extremely traditional in its thinking in this area, with a refusal of military service, when it was something the church would neither approve nor conceal? In fact when war broke out Councils of Brethren sent leaflets to the theologians in the barracks and trenches, in which it was laid down that wars were not the responsibility of the individual but of governments and that it was possible to be a soldier with a good conscience.[58] Bonhoeffer was certainly correct in writing to Bell in spring 1939 that ". . . the Confessing Church as a body has taken no definite stand on this point and probably cannot do so as things now are. So I would do my brethren great damage if I were to demonstrate my opposition on this point."[59]

Politically, there was a crisis in the army in February 1938 after the dismissal of General Werner Freiherr von Fritsch. On the military side the investigation was placed in the hands of Hans Oster, at that time head of the military security department of Admiral Wilhelm Canaris, and for the Minister of Justice, Franz Gürtner, the case was dealt with by his personal assistant, Hans von Dohnanyi. Oster and Dohnanyi soon found each other involved in the plan to use the Fritsch case to incite the military against Hitler. They conferred among others with General Ludwig Beck, who was later to become leader of the conspiracy against Hitler. Both of them were actively involved from then on in the various preparations for Hitler's

General Werner Freiherr von Fritsch, 1939

overthrow. Bonhoeffer found himself the close confidant of his brother-in-law, Dohnanyi. He was thus already an accessory to the plans and this in itself was a crime carrying the death penalty. Was the accessory to become an accomplice one day in the future?

Bonhoeffer put off the decision. At first he even considered emigration. Did he have to go on serving this country and this church? Could he not do his work on a theology of ethics, which he intended to write, far better outside in the ecumenical world, which was far more open to him than to most others? Was this not perhaps even the best way of serving his own church?

*

While Hitler was marching into Bohemia and Moravia in March 1939, Bonhoeffer was visiting his twin sister in exile in England and preparing for a further sabbatical in America with the help of Reinhold Niebuhr and Paul Lehmann. All doors were open to him: work, food and a

97

place in society, all that other emigrants often lacked, he found available and waiting for him.

The most difficult feat, that of his exemption from military service and the obtaining of a visa, was successfully accomplished. He set out, with a heavy heart, on 2 June 1939.

A moving journal of his time in New York has been preserved. It provides a window into the most onerous decision of his life, after which all further moves seem to take place as a matter of course: "Above all I miss Germany, and the brethren. The first lonely hours are difficult. I do not understand why I am here, whether it was wise, whether it will prove worthwhile ... Nearly two weeks have passed without any news of what is happening over there. It is almost unbearable."

The time of decision came for him on 20 June 1939. On the previous evening he wrote: "No news from Germany all day, waited in vain from one post to the next. No point in becoming angry ... I wish I knew how the work is going over there, whether everything is going well or whether I am needed. I wish I had a sign from over there to help me in the decisive talk tomorrow. Perhaps it is just as well that there is none."

The following evening he wrote: "Visit to Leiper [General Secretary of the Federal Council of Churches]. The decision has been taken. I have refused. It was obvious that he was disappointed and perhaps even offended. It has wider implications for me than I can foresee at the moment. Only God can know. It is extraordinary how I am never certain of my motives in any of my decisions. Is this a sign of confusion, of an inner dishonesty or is it a sign that we are being guided beyond what we can understand or is it perhaps both?"

The next day he wrote: "We cannot escape our destiny; least of all out here ... It is strange how strongly these particular thoughts occupy my mind these days and thoughts of the *Una Sancta* make little headway."

In a letter to Reinhold Niebuhr he said: "It was a mis-

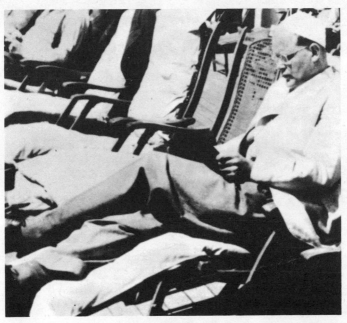

Crossing to New York, June 1939

take for me to come to America. I have to live through
this difficult period in our nation's history with Christians
in Germany. I will have no right to participate in the reconstruction of Christian life in Germany after the war if I
do not share the tribulations of this time with my people
. . . Christians in Germany are faced with the fearful alternatives either of willing their country's defeat so that
Christian civilization may survive, or of willing its victory
and destroying our civilization. I know which of the two
alternatives I have to choose but I cannot make the choice
from a position of safety."

Finally on 7 July he wrote: "The last day. Paul Lehmann tried to keep me here. To no avail. Journey to the
boat with Paul. Said goodbye at half-past eleven . . . My
travels are over. I am happy I went and happy to be going
home . . . at least I have had valuable insights which will

99

General Hans Oster   Hans von Dohnanyi

help me in any future personal decisions. I have probably
yet to feel the true influence the trip has had on me. Since
I came on board, my inner uncertainties about the future
have ceased. I can think about my shortened stay in America without regrets."[60]

*

At first, in spite of the outbreak of war, Bonhoeffer took
up his old work in Further Pomerania again, as though
there had been no interruption. When this was brought to
an end in March 1940, the Council of Brethren made him
and Eberhard Bethge, his assistant at Sigurdshof, Church
Visitors. Both travelled throughout the east Prussian parishes that summer. Meanwhile Bonhoeffer was let into the
secret of the unfortunately unsuccessful plans to overthrow Hitler before the war in the West intensified, plans
made by the group comprising Oster, Dohnanyi and Josef
Müller. France's rapid surrender, quite unforeseen by the
military experts, brought Hitler to the height of his pres-
tige. The announcement of the surrender reached Bonhoeffer and Bethge in the garden of a café near Tilsit.
    Soon afterwards the Gestapo moved again. A raid was
made during a youth conference in Bloestau near Königs-

berg, where Bonhoeffer was holding a Bible study group for students. Bonhoeffer was then banned from speaking in public on the grounds of "subversive activity", and had to report to the police regularly at his official place of residence, Schlawe in Further Pomerania. This considerably complicated his position.

After the Gestapo's intervention in Bloestau, Dohnanyi had intimated to his brother-in-law, at Oster's suggestion, that Military Intelligence were interested in his journeys near the border and the eastern front, and that as a precaution his next journey to the East could be protected from any interference. After the order to report to the police was imposed on 4 September, Canaris' security organization (the *Abwehr*) had Bonhoeffer declared indispensable for its work and so removed him from the jurisdiction of the Pomeranian police station. Oster and Dohnanyi put him on the staff of the Munich office as a civil employee of the *Abwehr*, as far away from Pomerania as possible. His way into the circle of active military resistance had begun. Bonhoeffer now had to register in Munich. He usually stayed in the Benedictine monastery at Ettal, where he worked on his *Ethics* and waited for *Abwehr* commissions which would allow him to travel abroad. One day in the cloister he was astonished to learn that the reading at the midday meal was to be taken from his book *Gemeinsames Leben* (Life Together).

Officially Bonhoeffer remained in the service of the Confessing Church, and did, in fact, work on several theological commissions set up by the Confessing Synods.

The Councils of Brethren, the "authorities" for him, had only rather imprecise information about Bonhoeffer's military assignments. These were dual-purpose: on the one hand he had to gather in foreign news as a screen, and at the same time he had to pass information abroad about the progress of German resistance. In addition he provided the conspirators with information about foreign friends. The leaders of the conspiracy found the excellent foreign contacts of a pastor highly regarded in ecumenical circles

101

Admiral Wilhelm Canaris

very useful. Their own credibility had been shattered since Hitler's conquest of half Europe had given the lie to their assurances that they would soon put an end to his activities. For his part Bonhoeffer was acutely conscious of the extraordinary situation in which he had placed himself by putting his ecumenical connections apparently at the disposal of the German military secret service but in reality, of course, at the disposal of the Resistance.

There was, however, no longer any question of going back; the step from accessory to conspirator had basically been taken when he returned home from America. Now the first deportations of Jews made the need for action even more urgent.

With his active involvement in conspiracy there was a change in Bonhoeffer's theological work. It was not a matter of his concentration diminishing. On the contrary: between official journeys there were whole periods of intensive and fruitful work on *Ethics*. He had always considered the conception of a new theological ethic as his major life work. Now it was really under way. And just as the Church struggle and *praxis pietatis* of Finkenwalde had provided the background to his work *The Cost of Discipleship*, so now the experiences of the conspiracy and its problems lay behind his new work.

*

On the affairs of the *Abwehr* and with the passport and visa facilities which it provided, he now undertook trips to Switzerland, Sweden, Norway and Italy. They fall into three stages.

Initially, in the spring of 1941 his task was to inform foreign friends about the continuing existence and work of the political underground organization, and to bring back information from abroad for his own group. So his journeys to Switzerland were totally taken up with cautious attempts to renew contacts. Bonhoeffer saw Sutz and Barth and Visser 't Hooft, the last of whom sent to London a detailed report about his visitor and the news he had brought.[61]

When Bonhoeffer returned home from the four-week visit, he was faced with Goebbels' proscription on the activities of all writers who were not members of the National Office for Literature. He let the matter rest at a few protests, for he had been aware for some time that he was writing without hope of publication. His actual work on *Ethics*, however, was not affected by it.

His second journey, in September 1941 and again to Switzerland, was intended as a reconnaissance of peace aims on the Allied side, especially those of responsible Christian leaders such as the Anglo-American peace groups. In order to make clear that an imminent change in Germany should be reckoned with and adjustment accordingly made, he wrote a critique of William Paton's newest book *The Church and the New Order*, in which he stated as much in guarded terms. Visser 't Hooft sent this as a memorandum with an accompanying letter to both the English and American Peace Aims Groups.[62] In London, however, little importance was attached to this communication about a possible overthrow of Hitler, and no reply was sent.

On returning home this time, he was greeted by the news of the first major deportations of Jews from Berlin. With his friend F. J. Perels, who was Legal Adviser to the Confessing Church, Bonhoeffer drew up a report for the opposition in the army command[63], in an attempt to hasten the *putsch*. In addition he helped Canaris in a bid to take a small group of Jews safely to Switzerland. At this point a severe attack of pneumonia brought an end to his work for several weeks.

During the third stage, at the end of May 1942, he met his old friend George Bell, the Bishop of Chichester, in Sweden, being commissioned to give Bell precise details (even the names of those involved) of an impending *putsch*. The English government were asked that, if these names figured in a *coup d'état*, they should give the leaders of the *putsch* time and space to establish a new government. Bell's information was communicated to Eden, the Foreign Minister, but led to nothing: Eden refused to send any answer at all to the conspirators. Although he had no doubts about the integrity of the actual informants, Bonhoeffer and Schönfeld, it might none the less have been a cloak for peace-feelers put out by the Nazis. Bell was persuaded, with difficulty, to let the matter drop. In the spring of 1943 he at last had an opportunity to raise in the House of Lords, the question of whether the British Government was prepared to make a distinction between Nazis and Germans. He had no idea that at precisely the same time the *putsch* was being set in motion with an assassination attempt in which the bomb (carried by Fabian von Schlabrendorff) failed to go off. Bonhoeffer and Dohnanyi were both involved in this attempt.

George Bell and Franz Hildebrandt in front of St Martin-in-the-Fields, London, after the Service of Intercession for Martin Niemöller, 1 July 1941

Before his trip to Sweden, Bonhoeffer had in April been to Norway with Helmuth von Moltke – both ostensibly on one of Canaris' missions – to give encouragement to the church resistance which had flared up anew there, and in particular to the measures taken by Bishop Eivind Berggrav. As a result of his visit to Sweden, in June Bonhoeffer went to Rome with his brother-in-law Dohnanyi, in the vain hope of obtaining a reply from London through the Vatican.

Not long afterwards the situation for both him and Dohnanyi began to become precarious.

*

Both men now received warnings that they were under surveillance, that their telephones were being tapped and that it might come to house searches. The impetus for such moves came, however, not from the conspiratorial actions of the last few months but from a totally different direction. Himmler and the Reich Security Office had for some time been anxious to incorporate the military security at Tirpitz-Ufer into their headquarters in Prinz-Albrecht-Strasse. Those in power in Prinz-Albrecht-Strasse were therefore anxious for any evidence of inefficiency at Tirpitz-Ufer and immediately pounced when the Prague customs-search office attributed foreign currency irregularities to a man who claimed to be acting for Consul Schmidhuber in Munich. Schmidhuber was one of Bonhoeffer's superiors in the Munich office of the *Abwehr*; he was arrested in October 1942. Schmidhuber knew of the transportation of the group of Jews to Switzerland and the arrangements for passport and foreign currency for them; he was informed about the special position Bonhoeffer occupied in the *Abwehr*. He knew little detail about what the latter had in fact achieved on his journeys abroad, for Bonhoeffer reported on this direct to the Berlin headquarters at Tirpitz-Ufer. Nevertheless, in the Schmidhuber case the investigations were extended to include the Berlin central office. Now everything depended on whether the chief of the Army High Command, Wilhelm Keitel, gave permission for an investigation to take place there and approved the disclosure of *Abwehr* activities. If it were done, then the Reich Security Office was furnished with a welcome opportunity to examine Canaris' office thoroughly, to play people off against one another and finally to curtail the independence of the *Abwehr*. Canaris was ready to shield Dohnanyi, Bonhoeffer and Müller. But through Schmidhuber's interrogations their names had already been noted in Prinz-Albrecht-Strasse.

During the tug of war with Keitel over approval for the interrogation of *Abwehr* personnel, for house searches and even arrests, the three who were in danger prepared for any eventuality. When they had just been reassured again by Canaris that the case would not go to court nor to the Gestapo, the blow fell.

On 5 April 1943 Bonhoeffer tried to telephone his sister Christine von Dohnanyi from his parents' house. A man's voice answered. At once he thought: that means either a house search or arrests. His parents were having an afternoon rest. He went next door to discuss the situation with his sister Ursula Schleicher, and to eat the good meal that she prepared for him in case he was later arrested. Then he checked his untidy desk to make sure that there was the right mixture of theology and camouflage material[64] and went back to his sister's house to wait with her and her family and Eberhard Bethge. At about four o'clock the black Mercedes turned into the little cul-de-sac and shortly afterwards his father came to fetch him, with the news that two men wanted to speak to him.

Not long afterwards Judge Advocate Dr Manfred Roeder and Detective Sonderegger from the Gestapo drove off with him. Dietrich Bonhoeffer was never to see the Marienburger Allee again.

*

In January of that year Bonhoeffer had become engaged to Maria von Wedemeyer, the granddaughter of Frau

Maria von Wedemeyer, 1942

Ruth von Kleist-Retzow of Klein-Krössin in Further Pomerania, and a cousin of Fabian von Schlabrendorff, whom Bonhoeffer had met at the house of Ewald von Kleist. She was eighteen years old, very beautiful, bright and lively. Most of their relatives first heard of the engagement only after Bonhoeffer had been taken to Tegel prison.

It was not the first time that Bonhoeffer had been in love. Towards the end of the twenties and the early thirties he had had a close woman friend, who was also a theologian and to whom he had sent every one of his sermons from London. Then the relationship came to an end. During the period of the House of Brethren he had no wish to bind anyone else to the fate that he saw in store for any man of the Church at that time, and he also wanted to remain free himself to act whatever might happen. Now there had been many changes; it was not less dangerous, quite the contrary. But half out of defiance of the current feelings of doom, and half out of a new mature

With Ruth von Kleist-Retzow in Kieckow (Pomerania), summer 1942

openness towards the earth-bound but good gifts of love and family, he had given his thoughts and feelings free play since the summer of 1942 and, after some inner hesitation, had accepted them joyfully when he discovered that his chosen partner was not insensible to them.

A year later Bonhoeffer was to write to Eberhard Bethge in a letter smuggled out of his cell in Tegel (22 December 1943): "Now I want to assure you that I haven't for a moment regretted coming back in 1939 – nor any of the consequences either. I knew quite well what I was doing, and I acted with a clear conscience. I've no wish to cross out of my life anything that has happened since, either to me personally (would I have got engaged otherwise? Would you have married? not to mention Sigurdshof, East Prussia, Ettal, my illness and all the help you gave me then, and the time in Berlin), or as regards events in general. And I regard my being kept here (do you remember that I prophesied to you last March about what the year would bring?) as being involved in the fate of Germany in which I was determined to share. I look back on the past without any self-reproach and accept the present in the same spirit."[65]

*

Obviously it is impossible to chart the way into the conspiracy from any literary or theological point of view: a conspiracy permits of no detailed papers which might be found and prove treacherous. Also, Bonhoeffer's conspiring would have been lacking in seriousness if he had worked out a vindication for it nervously beforehand. Vindication before whom? The Confessing Church? The Ecumenical Movement? What would have entitled them to expect such a thing?

None the less there are written indicators which mark the turns which led Bonhoeffer from non-violent resistance, through an attempt to withdraw, and on to an active part in the plot. As time passed, his feeling of guilt because he had opted out of responsibility became ever clearer and more intolerable. So he too faced up to what up until then his brothers, brothers-in-law and friends had undertaken without him. This new attitude altered his perception of reality – and this was to lead to a renewal of his theological perception of Christ.

First he noticed in himself a change both in his experience and in his language. On 25 June 1942 he wrote to Eberhard Bethge while travelling to Munich: "My recent very active and very worldly life has been giving me cause for reflection again and again. I am surprised that I can and do live for days without the Bible – if I were to force myself to read it, I would regard it as auto-suggestion not obedience. I can understand how such auto-suggestion can be and is a great help but I am afraid of falsifying a genuine experience and finally not experiencing the genuine help. When I once again open the Bible I find it new and enriching as never before and I long to preach once again . . . But I sense a growing abhorrence in me of all 'religiosity', often it is practically an instinctive repugnance – which is certainly not good either. I am not religious by nature. But I cannot stop thinking of God and Christ, the concepts of genuineness, life, freedom and mercy are dear to me. Only I find their religious garb repugnant. Do you understand? These thoughts and insights are far from new, but I think that a knot will be broken if I let things take their course and am not on my guard . . . In this sense I even understand my present work in the secular sphere."[66]

In his work on *Ethics*, too, there are reflections which reveal their obvious connection with his experiences at the time and his analysis of them. It contains, for instance, a portrait of Hitler: ". . . it is easy for the tyrannical despiser of men to exploit the baseness of the human heart, nurturing it and calling it by other names. Fear he calls responsibility. Desire he calls keenness. Dependency becomes solidarity. Brutality becomes masterfulness. Human weaknesses are played upon with unchaste seductiveness, so that meanness and baseness are reproduced and multiplied

111

ever anew. . . . As the base man grows baser, he becomes an ever more willing and adaptable tool in the hand of the tyrant. The small band of the upright are reviled. Their bravery is called revolt; their discipline is called pharisaism; their independence arbitrariness and their masterfulness arrogance. For the tyrannical despiser of men popularity is the token of the highest love of mankind. His secret profound mistrust for all human beings he conceals behind words stolen from a true community . . . He thinks people stupid, and they become stupid. He thinks them weak, and they become weak. He thinks them criminal, and they become criminal . . . In his profound contempt for his fellow-men he seeks the favour of those whom he despises, and the more he does so the more certainly he promotes the deification of his own person by the mob."[67]

During the same weeks in the autumn of 1940 when Bonhoeffer made up his mind to join the conspiracy, in his *Ethics* he described his church's guilt in the situation – less emotively, but more analytically and concretely than the Confessing Church put it in its famous confession of guilt at Stuttgart in 1945: "The Church . . . was silent when it should have cried out because the blood of the innocent was crying aloud to heaven. . . . It has stood by while violence and wrong were being committed under cover of . . . the name of Jesus Christ . . . The Church confesses that it has witnessed the lawless application of brute force, the physical and spiritual suffering of countless innocent people, oppression, hatred and murder, and that it has not raised its voice on behalf of the victims and has not found ways to hasten to their aid. It is guilty of the deaths of the weakest and most defenceless brothers of Jesus Christ [he means the Jews]. . . . The Church confesses that it has witnessed in silence the spoliation and exploitation of the poor and the enrichment and corruption of the strong. The Church confesses itself guilty towards the countless victims of calumny, denunciation and defamation. It has not convicted the slanderer of his wrong-doing, and it has thereby abandoned the slandered to his fate."[68]

The monastery at Ettal

And any act itself rests on insight, according to *Ethics*: "The extraordinary necessity appeals to the freedom of the men who are responsible. There is now no law behind which the responsible man can seek cover, and there is, therefore, also no law which can compel the responsible man to take any particular decision in the face of such necessities. In this situation there can only be a complete renunciation of every law, together with the avowal that here one must make one's decision as a free venture, together also with the open admission that here the law is being infringed and violated and that necessity obeys no commandment. Precisely in this breaking of the law the validity of the law is acknowledged, and in this renunciation of all law, and in this alone, one's own decision and deed are entrusted unreservedly to the divine governance of history . . . If any man tries to escape guilt in responsibility he detaches himself from the ultimate reality of human existence, and what is more he cuts himself off from the redeeming mystery of Christ's bearing guilt without sin and he has no share in the divine justification which lies upon this event."[69]

Besides such ethical and theological reflections there was

113

also the essay, carefully hidden away in the attic of his parents' house, in which he directly addressed his family and closest friends in the conspiracy and which he dedicated to them at Christmas 1942. Under the title *After Ten Years* he describes the spiritual situation of the group of conspirators. There are sections called "Civil Courage?", "No Ground Under Our Feet", "Of Success", "Contempt for Humanity?", "The Sense of Quality", "Insecurity and Death", "Are we still of any use?"[70] . . .

The language of the trained theologian is unmistakable. But equally unmistakable is the self-critical dialogue – not written for his professional colleagues – which went on within this circle of marked men. Written down not later as hindsight, but in the very midst of a situation with the future unforeseeable, this essay is one of the documents of the German resistance which will still be read when its organizational and constitutional plans have long been forgotten.

After a description of the failure of the rational man, of the moral fanatic, of the man of conscience and the man of duty, in the excerpt "Who Stands Fast?" he goes on to say "Here and there people flee from public altercation into the sanctuary of private virtuousness. But anyone who does this must shut his mouth and his eyes to the injustice around him. Only at the cost of self-deception can he keep himself pure from the contamination arising from responsible action. In spite of all that he does, what he leaves undone will rob him of his peace of mind. He will either go to pieces because of this disquiet, or become the most hypocritical of Pharisees."

In the passage on "Civil Courage?" Bonhoeffer is clearly describing himself for some of the time, his own attempt at total discipleship but put in secular terms: ". . . Who would deny that in obedience, in their task and calling, the Germans have again and again shown the utmost bravery and self-sacrifice? But the German has kept his freedom – and what nation has talked more passionately of freedom than the Germans, from Luther to the

114

idealist philosophers? – by seeking deliverance from self-will through service to the community. Calling and freedom were to him two sides of the same thing. But in this he misjudged the world; he did not realize that this submissiveness and self-sacrifice could be exploited for evil ends. When that happened, the exercise of the calling itself became questionable, and all the moral principles of the German were bound to totter. The fact could not be escaped that the German still lacked something fundamental: he could not see the need for free and responsible action, even in opposition to his task and his calling; in its place there appeared on the one hand an irresponsible lack of scruple, and on the other a self-tormenting punctiliousness that never led to action. Civil courage, in fact, can grow only out of the free responsibility of free men. Only now are the Germans beginning to discover the meaning of free responsibility."

In the passage headed "Of Folly" he shows himself, without having done much behaviourist research, as an intuitive psychologist: "Folly is a more dangerous enemy to the good than evil. One can protest against evil; it can be unmasked and, if need be, prevented by force. Evil always carries the seeds of its own destruction, as it makes people, at the least, uncomfortable. Against folly we have no defence. Neither protests nor force can touch it . . . A fool must therefore be treated more cautiously than a scoundrel; we shall never again try to reason with the fool, for it is both useless and dangerous . . . If we look more closely, we see that any violent display of power, whether political or religious, produces an outburst of folly in a large part of mankind . . ."

The essay finishes soberly and self-critically: "We have been silent witnesses of evil deeds. We have been drenched by many storms. We have learnt the arts of equivocation and pretence. Experience has made us suspicious of others, and kept us from being truthful and open. Intolerable conflicts have worn us down and even made us cynical. Are we still of any use?"[71]

115

8   *Prisons*

For Bonhoeffer life in a prison-cell in the Berlin suburb of Tegel was at first harrowing. As a prisoner who had no experience even of life in a barracks, Bonhoeffer really missed soap and fresh linen. He had practised living alone voluntarily often enough. But his situation now was different: first, complete solitary confinement. The guards were not allowed to talk to this "political" prisoner. What help were his accustomed spiritual exercises now? On a scrap of paper preserved from those early weeks are the words: "Suicide, not because of consciousness of guilt but because basically I am already dead, draw a line, summing up".[72] Tough and athletic as he was, he had always been afraid that he would not be able to withstand ill-treatment or tricks of interrogation and would perhaps betray friends who were still in a position to continue the conspiracy. Perhaps killing oneself was even a duty?

Such notes do not recur during the next period. But for a good quarter of a year the tension remained: would he be able throughout the interrogation to keep to the version of events which had previously been agreed with Hans von Dohnanyi and Josef Müller? The three prisoners were in different gaols but family and friends kept them informed with a laborious but successful system of reports on the current state of the interrogations and the possible intentions of the interrogators.

When the interrogation period was over, Bonhoeffer's cell at Tegel became a study. He had books, paper for writing, cigarettes, coffee and food, all provided by his fiancée and his family. Then the guards too enjoyed their share of the delicacies. Initially only the censored, officially permitted letters were brought out from the prison every ten days, but later there were also smuggled letters,

116

Bonhoeffer's cell in Tegel

The prison at Berlin-Tegel (X marks Bonhoeffer's first cell)

which were collected after the war to form a volume with the title *Widerstand und Ergebung* (Letters and Papers from Prison).

The family's skill in using old contacts and making new ones was unflagging. In addition, they were helped by the fact that Tegel was not a Gestapo prison – let alone a concentration camp – but a military prison, in which professional soldiers no longer fit for action at the front were used as guards. Among them were some very sympathetic towards the interesting and generous prisoner, who did all they could for him as soon as the solitary confinement rule was relaxed. In addition, Berlin military prisons were at that time under the jurisdiction of a cousin of Bonhoeffer's mother, Lieutenant General Paul von Hase, the city commandant. Hase himself was involved in the *Putsch* and was executed immediately after 20 July 1944.

When the prison commandant and his guards learned who the prisoner's relatives were, their respect for him increased. Half-amused, half-disgusted, Bonhoeffer sketched the effect that General von Hase's enquiry about him produced: "After 12 days the authorities got to know of my family connections. While this was a great relief to me personally, it was most embarrassing to see how everything changed from that moment. I was put into a more spacious cell, which one of the men cleaned every day for me; I was offered larger rations, which I always refused, as they would have been at the expense of the other prisoners; the captain fetched me for a daily walk, with the result that the staff treated me with studied politeness – in fact, several of them came to apologize: 'We didn't know', etc. It was painful." And three weeks before the *Putsch* attempt: "Uncle Paul has been here. He had me brought downstairs at once, and stayed – Maetz and Maass [the prison commandants] were there – more than five hours! He had four bottles of Sekt brought – a unique event in the annals of this place."[73] For the prison warders the inmate of the solitary confinement cell had become a star detainee.

This was useful in itself, but did not alter the severity and danger of the actual hearings, since Keitel had now given permission for the judicial examination to proceed. This was conducted by Judge Advocate Manfred Roeder, who was attached to the Luftwaffe, in the presence of Sonderegger, a Gestapo official. Roeder had earlier concluded the so-called *Rote Kapelle* trial with death sentences on Arvid Harnack, his wife Mildred and Harro Schulze-Boysen, who also belonged to the Luftwaffe, and now there was considerable eagerness to cast a slur on the army section, the *Wehrmacht*, of which the *Abwehr* was part.

The investigations were principally concerned with Dohnanyi. The Judge Advocate had a far from easy task with him since he was a lawyer and a colleague; in fact, Roeder did not manage to achieve his aims. Bonhoeffer had consciously to play along with him. He had the advantage of being able to pretend he was a complete novice in the matters in which Roeder was interested. For example, according to his own account written in the cell, Bonhoeffer assured Roeder: "I am the last person to want to dispute that in an activity as strange and new to me as *Abwehr* service, and as complicated, mistakes could creep in . . . I often find it difficult to follow the tempo of your questioning, probably because I am not used to it."[74]

Before events took a turn for the worse after the disastrous failure of 20 July, Bonhoeffer always considered that any trial stood a good chance of concluding with a verdict favourable to him. Everything seemed well-concealed. His letters from Tegel, therefore, often have a surprisingly optimistic tone.

*

The proceedings against Bonhoeffer divide into three distinct stages during his stay in Tegel.

The first phase of Roeder's hearing, which concluded with the filing of the charge, lasted from April to July 1943.

The enquiries embraced four areas: (1) Bonhoeffer's exemption from normal military service and his position with the *Abwehr* security office which had enabled him to escape the scrutiny of the state police and continue with his church work; (2) "Operation 7", the travel arrangements for the Jewish group (originally seven in number) to reach Switzerland, to which a woman colleague of Bonhoeffer's in the Confessing Church had also been party; (3) his trips abroad, which had little to do with military intelligence; (4) his role as intermediary in enlisting for the *Abwehr* the help of other members of the Confessing Church, such as Niesel (who had an important position in the Council of Brethren), Bethge and others.

In his cell Bonhoeffer made a great many plans for and notes on these hearings and these have been preserved.[75] From them it is evident that he often successfully referred to Canaris' responsibility, as had already been agreed beforehand. He also referred to his own devotion to the State and, as additional camouflage, supported this with

Lieut.-General
Paul von Hase,
Commanding
Officer, Berlin

In Tegel prison yard.
Sergeant-Major
Napp with
Bonhoeffer and four
Italian prisoners,
late summer 1944

Nächtliche Stimmen

"Night Voices", the poem written in Tegel

quotations from his theological writings. He refers, for instance, to *The Cost of Discipleship*: "If anyone wants to learn something of my conception of the duty of Christian obedience towards the authorities, he should read my exposition of Romans 13 in my book *The Cost of Discipleship*. The appeal to subjection to the will and the demands of authority for the sake of Christian conscience has probably seldom been expressed more strongly than there."[76]

Ich höre, ich höre,
die Stimmen, die Rufe,
die Schreie nach rettenden Planken,
der wachenden, träumenden Leidensgefährten
hilfleich umdunkle Gedanken.
Ich hör unruhiges Knarren der Betten,
ich höre Ketten.

Ich höre, wie Männer sich schlaflos werfen und dehnen,
die sich nach Freiheit u. zornigen Taten sehnen.
Wenn der Schlaf sie heimsucht in den Mitternachtsstunden,
murmeln sie träumend von Kindern u. Frauen.
Ich höre glückliches Lispeln halbwachsener Knaben,
die sich an kindlichen Träumen laben.
Ich hör sie zerren an ihren flatternden Decken
und sich vor gräßlichen Albträumen verstecken.
Ich höre Seufzen u. schwaches Atmen der Greise,
die sich im Stillen bereiten zur frommen Reise.
Sie schön Recht u. Unrecht kommen u. gehn,
nun wollen sie unvergänglichen Frieden sehn.

The investigators had not succeeded in discovering facts
proving a conspiracy; therefore findings of high treason
and treason against his country could not be included in
the charge. All that remained was a charge of avoiding
military service by causing himself and others to be put on
the reserve list. This was a sufficiently serious charge, in
view of the harsh enlistment regulations brought into force
after the defeat at Stalingrad, but by no means as serious
as conspiracy. And it was up to Canaris, Oster and Doh-

nanyi to justify the exemptions, which they were ready and prepared to do.

Unwittingly the National Socialists had achieved success in one area: the Oster-Dohnanyi office, which until the beginning of 1943 had been the link in the *Abwehr* between the conspirators, and in particular the link with General Beck, had suddenly ceased to function. Its role was, however, taken over by the central information office of the home army under General Olbricht and Colonel Stauffenberg.

The second phase of Bonhoeffer's imprisonment in Tegel was dominated by preparations for the trial. It stretched on until April 1944. Repeatedly, new dates were fixed. Each time he prepared all over again; he suffered from the postponements. But his family and friends were chiefly preoccupied with the need to have Roeder removed from the case, and in the winter this was finally achieved through his promotion. Now the style of the enquiry changed noticeably: Roeder's successor, Kutzner, finally disclosed that he would no longer act in the case and would not press any charges. Bonhoeffer's friends considered this a great success, but it proved impossible to persuade Keitel to keep the Reich Security Office out of the case. So in April 1944 his friends sent word to Bonhoeffer that there was to be no trial; there was nothing to be done but to let the matter "silt up" (this was the expression used) until after the *putsch*.

In the third phase Bonhoeffer was therefore forced to drop his pressure for the case to be cleared up by a trial. In fact, a revival of interest on the part of Himmler, or even Hitler himself, seemed an incalculable risk. So he set himself to wait, and a new phase of work, the most fruitful of all, began in the prison cell. Indeed, some theologians regard Bonhoeffer's first great theological letter of 30 April 1944[77] as the beginning of a new theological epoch.

On the evening of 20 July he learned of the failure of the *putsch*. For some time he had had access to the sickbay in the prison, since he had been detailed to help with air raid alarms, and so was able to listen to the news, even to the BBC. On 21 July he gave up all hope and prepared himself for the worst.

He tried to adopt a fresh outlook and to turn his attention less to himself than to those outside and how they were to deal with this new setback and Hitler's new victory. On 21 July he wrote a letter to Eberhard Bethge (who was then on the Italian front), which was, as it happened, an account of his life and experiments.

"I expect you are often with us here in your thoughts and are always glad of any sign of life, even if the theological discussion stops for a moment. These theological thoughts are, in fact, always occupying my mind; but there are times when I am just content to live the life of faith without worrying about its problems. At those times I simply take pleasure in the day's readings – in particular those of yesterday and today. And I'm always glad to go back to Paul Gerhardt's beautiful hymns.

"During the last year or so I've come to know and understand more and more the profound this-worldliness of Christianity. The Christian is not a *homo religiosus*, but simply a man, as Jesus was man – in contrast, shall we say, to John the Baptist. I don't mean the shallow and banal this-worldliness of the enlightened, the busy, the comfortable, or the lascivious, but the profound this-worldliness, characterized by discipline and the constant knowledge of death and resurrection. I think Luther lived a this-worldly life in this sense.

"I remember a conversation that I had in America thirteen years ago with a young French pastor. We were asking ourselves quite simply what we wanted to do with our lives. He said he would like to become a saint (and I think it's quite likely that he did become one). At the time I was very impressed, but I disagreed with him, and said, in effect, that I should like to learn to have faith. For a long time I didn't realize the depth of the contrast. I thought I could acquire faith by trying to live a holy life, or something like it. I suppose I wrote *The Cost of Dis-*

In the Führer's headquarters: Hitler, Goering, Jodl, Keitel

cipleship as the end of that path. Today I can see the dangers of that book, though I still stand by what I wrote.

"I discovered later, and I'm still discovering right up to this moment, that it is only by living completely in this world that one learns to have faith. One must completely abandon any attempt to make something of oneself, whether it be a saint, or a converted sinner, or a churchman (a so-called priestly type!), a righteous man or an unrighteous one, a sick man or a healthy one. By this-worldliness I mean living unreservedly in life's duties, problems, successes and failures, experiences and perplexities. In so doing we throw ourselves completely into the arms of God, taking seriously, not our own sufferings, but those of God in the world – watching with Christ in Gethsemane. That, I think, is faith; that is *metanoia*; and that is how one becomes a man and a Christian (cf. Jer. 45:) . . . I'm glad to have been able to learn this, and I know I've been able to

126

do so only along the road that I've travelled. So I'm grateful for the past and present, and content with them."[78]

A few days after this very personal account he wrote a poem. In the meantime he had heard the news that Stauffenberg and his companions had been shot in the yard of the Bendlerblock (among those killed was the brother of his friend Werner von Haeften, who had been in his confirmation classes long ago), and had also been informed of the death of his uncle, Paul von Hase.

STATIONS ON THE ROAD TO FREEDOM

Action

Daring to do what is right, not what fancy may tell you,
valiantly grasping occasions, not cravenly doubting –
freedom comes only through deeds, not through thoughts
   taking wing.
Faint not nor fear, but go out to the storm and the
   action,
trusting in God whose commandment you faithfully
   follow;
freedom, exultant, will welcome your spirit with joy.

Suffering

A change has come indeed. Your hands, so strong and
   active,
are bound; in helplessness now you see your action
is ended; you sigh in relief, your cause committing
to stronger hands; so now you may rest contented.
Only for one blissful moment could you draw near to
   touch freedom;
then, that it might be perfected in glory, you gave it to
   God.

Death

Come now, thou greatest of feasts on the journey to freedom eternal;
death, cast aside all the burdensome chains, and demolish

the walls of our temporal body, the walls of our soul that
   are blinded,
so that at last we may see that which here remains
   hidden.
Freedom, how long we have sought thee in discipline,
   action and suffering;
dying, we now may behold thee revealed in the Lord.[79]

The awaited summons from the Gestapo failed to come.
Days then weeks went by.

Initially, Hitler had executed immediately all those who
were arrested in connection with the plot of 20 July, which
meant that the authorities could not use them to uncover
further circles in the conspiracy. In Tegel Bonhoeffer now
started to consider seriously the until then only vaguely
formulated plan for escaping and going underground. His
guard, Corporal Knobloch, a North Berlin working-man,
who had also passed on his secret correspondence, was
ready to make a run for it, with Bonhoeffer disguised as a
mechanic. On 24 September the Schleichers and their
daughter Renate (now married to Eberhard Bethge) on
Bonhoeffer's instructions drove to Berlin-Niederschönhau-
sen and left mechanic's clothing, ration cards and money
at some allotments. A week later, however, Klaus Bonhoeffer and Rüdiger Schleicher were arrested for their part
in the plot, and Eberhard Bethge was imprisoned at the
end of October. Dietrich Bonhoeffer therefore abandoned
his escape plan, so as not to endanger his brother, brother-
in-law, parents and fiancée even further.

Meanwhile the Gestapo had made one of their most
important finds. Documents, which proved the involvement of Oster, Dohnanyi and Bonhoeffer in the conspiracy from as early as 1938, were discovered in a safe in the
Abwehr emergency headquarters at Zossen near Berlin.
Hitler was beside himself. He countermanded the order for
the immediate liquidation of those conspirators already
arrested, in order to allow the further ramifications of the
conspiracy to be investigated more thoroughly. This ex-

Rüdiger Schleicher (1895–1945) Klaus Bonhoeffer (1901–45)

plains the long delays before the execution of Carl Goerdeler and many others, among them Bonhoeffer and Dohnanyi.

On Sunday 8 October 1944 a Gestapo commando unit appeared and removed Bonhoeffer from the military prison at Tegel to the basement prison at Prinz-Albrecht-Strasse.

*

At the Reich Security Head Office a new series of cross-examinations started, different in every respect from the preceding ones.

Secret messages and visitors no longer reached Bonhoeffer. His previous helpers – F. J. Perels, the military judge Dr Karl Sack, who had been the most important source of advice and manipulation in the military justice machine during the Tegel interrogations, Canaris and Oster – were all now only a few cells away from him, also being subjected to gruelling cross-examination. In addition, there was now no hope of any overthrow, which would have made the period of endurance more bearable.

Even now, however, there was some hope. The lawyer in charge of the interrogations, Walter Huppenkothen, had

Prison camp Flossenbürg

not only the task of investigating the conspiracy. He was also intended to probe where possible the as yet unexplored areas of the conspirators' foreign connections – ecumenical in Bonhoeffer's case – of which the Secret Service might be able to make good use, now that the military *Abwehr* security office had finally been incorporated into the Reich Security Head Office. Consequently Huppenkothen was collecting the dates of the conspiracy, under conditions of stringent secrecy, to complete the "Führer's file" being compiled on those newly implicated by the discovery of the Zossen documents. At the same time he was accumulating all the worthwhile information he could about Bonhoeffer's church connections abroad – so the later cross-examinations were more civilized in tone.

These enquiries are mentioned in a letter from Ernst Kaltenbrunner, the chief of the Reich Security Headquarters, to the Foreign Minister Joachim von Ribbentrop. The letter reports what Kaltenbrunner considered valuable news about English attitudes (Bell's political views, and those of Sir Stafford Cripps, Lord Beaverbrook, etc.) and other information obtained from the prisoner.[80]

While he was in the basement of the Headquarters, on the way to the shower Bonhoeffer had brief meetings in the corridors with friends such as Hans von Dohnanyi, Fabian von Schlabrendorff, Hans Böhm, Carl Goerdeler and others. Survivors like Schlabrendorff report that while Bonhoeffer was there he was also able to find out that the true extent of their conspiracy had still not been completely discovered.

At any rate Bonhoeffer was now counted important enough to be relegated to the group saved from execution for further interrogation. He was therefore given a place in a special convoy taking prominent prisoners to the concentration camp at Buchenwald on 7 February 1945, after several daytime air raids had caused severe damage in Prinz-Albrecht-Strasse.

Meanwhile Klaus Bonhoeffer and Rüdiger Schleicher had been sentenced to death by Roland Freisler's People's Court, although their actual execution had been postponed. In Buchenwald Dietrich Bonhoeffer was kept in a specially adapted cellar outside the camp, together with Josef Müller, Hermann Pünder, General Alexander von Falkenhausen, Molotov's nephew Wassili Kokorin, the English officers Captain S. Payne Best, Hugh Falconer and others. He shared a cell with General von Rabenau, who after his retirement had been a student of theology. On 1 April 1945 for the first time the prisoners in their cells heard the thunder of cannons from the river Werra. On 3 April they were put into a lorry and taken to Regensburg and Schönberg in the Bavarian forest. Falconer later reported to the family that Bonhoeffer "did a great deal to keep some of the weaker brethren from depression and anxiety. He spent a good deal of time with Wassili Kokorin, Molotov's nephew, who was a delightful young man although an atheist. I think your brother divided his time with him between instilling the foundations of Christianity and learning Russian."[81]

On 5 April 1945 during Hitler's midday conference the decision was taken: the "Zossen" group, among whom were Oster, Canaris, Dohnanyi and now Bonhoeffer, were not to survive. On 6 April Huppenkothen drove to the Sachsenhausen concentration camp for a court martial of Dohnanyi. On 7 April he went to the Flossenburg concentration camp, to which the S.S. Judge Thorbeck had already been ordered from Nuremburg. On 8 April and

Flossenbürg: Remains of the execution block

during the following night Canaris, Oster, Sack, Gehre and Strünck were all court martialled and sentenced to death. Where was Bonhoeffer? It was established that through an oversight he had been put on the transport lorry to the south-east. He had to be brought back.

On Low Sunday, 8 April, Bonhoeffer had held a service for his fellow-prisoners in the school at Schönberg. At about noon the men sent by Huppenkothen appeared at the door, called him out alone, and transported him 150 kilometres northwards again. They arrived at Flossenbürg during the night and everything was handled very quickly. Then in the grey dawn of 9 April Bonhoeffer and his friends were hanged.

Hans von Dohnanyi was probably also put to death on 9 April in Sachsenhausen. Klaus Bonhoeffer and Rüdiger Schleicher were brought from their prison in the Lehrter Strasse on the night of 23 April and shot by an S.S. raiding squad. Eberhard Bethge, whose trial was intended to take place in May, was set free when the Soviet troops reached Berlin.

Bishop Bell has told how Payne Best brought him Dietrich's last greetings. When the guards arrived in Schönberg, Bonhoeffer said to Best: "Tell the Bishop that for me this is the end but also the beginning. With him [the Bishop] I believe in the principle of our Universal Christian brotherhood which rises above all national interests, and that our victory is certain."[82]

*

A vast number of letters and sketches date from Bonhoeffer's time in prison.

Apart from the censored letters to his parents, which were initially his sole link with the outside world, there are letters to his fiancée (both official and later smuggled ones too) which today are still under lock and key. There are in addition slips of paper with notes on the interrogations and rough drafts of letters to Roeder who was in charge of the investigations, as well as literary texts both of a theological and of a fictional nature (among them fragments of an attempt to write a novel and a play), memoranda on the prison situation and the bomb alerts intended for the attention of the commandant and of Paul von Hase, sermons for marriages and christenings, as well as prayers and meditations. And finally there are the smuggled letters to Eberhard Bethge, containing the theological passages which have since caused such a stir of interest throughout the world.

The go-between for the smuggled letters was the kindly Corporal Knobloch, of whom unfortunately nothing was heard after the Soviet entry into Berlin. This contact was one never discovered by the Gestapo. Bethge, however, destroyed Bonhoeffer's last letters, written in September 1944, before he himself was arrested. The greater part of the correspondence, which did not start until after the end of Roeder's interrogation when the danger of his friend being drawn into the case had become slight, has been preserved.

Seven years later the first selection of letters was published. They grant us an insight into the exceedingly rich intellectual world of a sensitive man engaged in a struggle, a great Christian, still capable of joy even within the narrow confines of a prison cell. The reactions of political prisoners the world over show a very similar sequence: at first every effort is made to convince oneself and one's family how well one is coming to terms with the unfamiliar situation.[83] But then later, in the first smuggled letters to his friend, the other, the darker side is expressed. So on 15 December 1943 Bonhoeffer wrote: "And then at last I should have to start telling you that, in spite of everything I've written so far, things here are revolting, that my grim experiences often pursue me into the night and that I can shake them off only by reciting one hymn after another, and that I'm apt to wake up with a sigh rather than with a hymn of praise to God. It's possible to get used to physical hardships, and to live for months out of the body, so to speak – almost too much so – but one doesn't get used to the psychological strain; on the contrary, I have the feeling that everything that I see and hear is putting years on me, and I'm often finding the world nauseating and burdensome."[84]

His fiancée, Maria von Wedemeyer, was a source of both joy and pain; he wrote to his friend on 15 December 1943: "We've now been engaged almost a year, and so far we haven't spent even an hour alone together. Isn't that mad! . . . We have to talk and write about things which in the end aren't the most important for the two of us; every month we sit upright for an hour, side by side, as on a school bench, and then we're torn apart again. We know almost nothing about each other, we haven't experienced anything together, even these months we experience in separation. Maria thinks I am a model of virtue, an exemplary Christian and, in order to set her at ease, I have to write letters like an elderly martyr, and her image of me becomes more and more false. Isn't that an impossible situation for her? And she bears up with such great self-control." In the last letter to Maria von Wedemeyer at Christmas 1944, handed over by Commissar Sonderegger, he wrote: "These will be quiet days in our homes. But I have had the experience over and over again that the quieter it is around me, the clearer do I feel the connection to you. It is as though in solitude the soul develops senses which we hardly know in everyday life. Therefore I have not felt lonely or abandoned for one moment . . . You must not think that I am unhappy. What is happiness and unhappiness? It depends so little on the circumstances; it depends really only on that which happens inside a person. I am grateful every day that I have you, and that makes me happy."[85]

In a letter written on 18 December 1943, he answered a problem his friend had raised after his army leave, the problem of reconciling the fear of death and the longing to live with the demands of piety: "I believe we ought so to love and trust God in our *lives*, and in all the good things that he sends us, that when the time comes (but not before!) we may go to him with love, trust, and joy. But, to put it plainly, for a man in his wife's arms to be hankering after the other world is, in mild terms, a piece of bad taste, and not God's will. We ought to find and love God in what he actually gives us; if it pleases him to allow us to enjoy some overwhelming earthly happiness, we mustn't try to be more pious than God himself and allow our happiness to be corrupted by presumption and arrogance, and by unbridled religious fantasy which is never satisfied with what God gives. God will see to it that the man who finds him in his earthly happiness and thanks him for it does not lack reminder that earthly things are transient, that it is good for him to attune his heart to what is eternal, and that sooner or later there will be times when he can say in all sincerity, 'I wish I were home'. But everything has its time, and the main thing is that we keep step with God, and do not keep pressing on a few steps ahead – nor keep dawdling a step behind. It's presumptuous to want to have everything at once – matrimonial bliss, the cross, and the heavenly Jerusalem."[86]

From his own experience of separation he now began to evolve new variations on the theme of longing, the lengthy and painful period of tension, the capacity for living in more than one dimension, and the necessity not to opt out of the present. He constantly put himself in the position of his friend on the Italian front. On 18 December 1943 and at Pentecost the following year he wrote: "Some people have been so violently shaken in their lives from their earliest days that they cannot now, so to speak, allow themselves any great longing or put up with a long period of tension, and they find compensation in short-lived pleasures that offer readier satisfaction. That is the fate of the proletarian classes, and it is the ruin of all intellectual fertility . . . Substitutes repel us; we simply have to wait and wait; we have to suffer unspeakably from the separation, and feel the longing till it almost makes us ill. That is the only way, although it is a very painful one, in which we can preserve unimpaired our relationship with our loved ones . . . I notice repeatedly here how few people there are who can harbour conflicting emotions at the same time. When bombers come, they are all fear; when there is something nice to eat, they are all greed; when they are disappointed, they are all despair; when they are successful, they can think of nothing else. They miss the fullness of life and the wholeness of an independent existence; everything objective and subjective is dissolved for them into fragments. By contrast, Christianity puts us into many different dimensions of life at the same time; we make room in ourselves, to some extent, for God and the whole world. We rejoice with those who rejoice, and weep with those who weep; we are anxious . . . about our life, but at the same time we must think about things much more important to us than life itself . . . What a deliverance it is to be able to *think*, and thereby remain multidimensional. I've almost made it a rule here, simply to tell people who are trembling under an air raid that it would be much worse for a small town. We have to get people

out of their one-track minds; that is a kind of 'preparation' for faith, or something that makes faith possible, although really it's only faith itself that can make possible a
multi-dimensional life, and so enable us to keep this Whit-
suntide, too, in spite of the alarms."[87]

Dietrich Bonhoeffer did his utmost for many of those
living within the walls of Tegel, both fellow-prisoners and
guards; he also immersed himself in the riches of literature,
secular rather than theological. He spoke of his enforced
idleness as "an unexpected sabbatical term".

Whenever he could, he tried to use his connections and
advantages for the benefit of others, not only by means of
the memoranda on prison conditions and alarm regulations already mentioned, but in other ways as well. He
drafted letters of complaint for fellow-prisoners, and
obtained psychiatric opinions for their defence lawyers
through his father; he provided money. With the sick and
after the alerts he acted as a skilled orderly and stretcher-
bearer. At Christmas he wrote prayers for the entire
prison, which the prison chaplain was able to distribute.
Naturally he tried to share in the family celebrations, the
wedding and the christening, as wholeheartedly as was
possible amidst all the misery. And even after confessing
to his friend that, in fact, life in the cell was not so easy to
bear as he made it seem in his letters, he finished his description on a humorous note: "Yes, I would tell you all
this and much more, and would know that (provided you
were not just reading a newspaper or sleeping or even thinking of Renate!) you would listen to me like no one else
and would give me good counsel."[88]

In addition to theology he read philosophy, history and
nineteenth-century literature more concentratedly than ever
before. Of course, in Tegel Bonhoeffer too was affected by
the isolation suffered by all educated people in National
Socialist Germany: for instance, under no circumstances could he risk having books by Thomas Mann, Franz
Werfel or any Socialist writers in his cell. The authors
who were allowed held few attractions for him and

his family. He wrote in a letter: "Unfortunately Maria's generation [she was then just nineteen years old] has grown up with a very bad kind of contemporary literature and finds it much harder than we did to take up earlier writing. The more we have come up against the really good things, the more insipid the weak lemonade of more recent productions has become to us, sometimes almost to the point of making us ill. Can you think of a book from the belles-lettres of, say, the last fifteen years which you think has lasting value? I can't. It is partly just talk, partly striking attitudes, partly plaintive sentimentality – no insight, no ideas, no clarity, no substance and almost always bad, unfree writing. At this point I am quite determinedly a *laudator temporis acti*."[89]

Since he could not participate in the literary development taking place in the outside world, Bonhoeffer took upon himself the task of renewing his acquaintance with the time and thought of writers from Keller to Harnack, Pestalozzi to Dilthey. His most enjoyable discovery was Adalbert Stifter: "The intimate life of his characters – of course it is old-fashioned of him to describe only likeable people – is very pleasant in this atmosphere here, and makes one think of the things that really matter in life ... The purity of its style and character-drawing gives one a quite rare and peculiar feeling of happiness."[90] *Witiko*, in particular, was an experience of fundamental importance for him, especially because it shows, as Hermann Bahr put it in 1922, a new justice springing from a good injustice and "the victory of illegal justice over a law that had become unjust".

During the weeks when he was reading *Witiko*'s one thousand pages he was also writing the draft of a drama. In it he gives the main character the words: "Let us learn to do what is right for a while without talking about it ... A man who knows himself close to death is resolute but also silent. Speechless, even, if it must be so, misunderstood and lonely, he does what is necessary and right, he brings his sacrifice ...

(Auf Eichberger Papierfabrik 4b, Konzeptpapier)

Der Alarm am 26.Nov. hat im Revier des WUG Tegel zu folgenden
Erfahrungen geführt. Bereits durch eine der ersten in der Nähe
fallenden Bomben wurden sämtliche Fenster und Verdunklungsvorrich-
tungen des Reviers zerstört, stürzten aus dem Arzneischrank meh-
rere Gefässe mit Arzeneien, der Fussboden war mit Staub und Trüm-
mern bedeckt, der Versuch, die Verdunkelung behelfsmässig instand
zu setzen, scheiterte, da immer neue Bomben-finsterneinschläge folg-
ten. Als kurz danach in etwa 25 m Entfernung eine Sprengbombe oder
Luftmine die Gefängnismauer einriss, Türen, Fenster und Dachbe-
deckung des WUG schwer beschädigte, erhob sich aus den Zellen der
eingeschlossenen U.-Gefangenen ein wildes An-die-Türen-schlagen,
Schreien, um Hilfe rufen von Verwundeten. Bei dem allgemeinen Lärm
der dadurch entstand, abgesehen von den Bombeneinschlägen war es
kaum möglich, festzustellen, wo wirklich Verwundete waren. Die
Revierbelegschaft öffnete einige Zellen und stellte kleine Ver-
wundungen fest, eine sofortige Behandlung aber war unmöglich, da
das Revier ohne Beleuchtung war, und wäre auch bei schwersten Ver-
wundungen nicht möglich gewesen. Erst nach dem Beschuss konnten
die Verdunkelung instandgesetzt und mit der Behandlung begonnen
werden. Eine noch schwerere Beschädigung des Reviers würde eine
Behandlung fast ganz unmöglich machen, da die an zwei anderen Stel
len des Hauses deponierten Verbandskästen für eine grosse Zahl von
Verletzten nicht ausreichen würde.
   Daraus ergeben sich folgende Konsequenzen: 1.) soll eine ärztl.
Versorgung in Ernstfällen gewährleistet sein, so ist die Anlage
eines Sanitätsbunkers erforderlich. 2.) Sanitätsdienstgrade unter
den U-Häftlingen sind bei Alarm nach Möglichkeit zur Dienstleistung
im Revier auszuschliessen. 3.) es sind Massnahmen erforderlich,
die es ermöglichen, die Verwundeten sofort ausfindig zu machen,
was bei dem gegenwärtigen Zustand nicht möglich ist. Wenn die
Sicherung des Lebens der leitende Gesichtspunkt ist, so wäre eine
möglichst weitgehende Ausschliessung der U-Häftlinge aus ihren
Zellen und die sofortige Herstellung von Splittergräben erforderlich. 4.) Auch die ungünstige seelische Auswirkung auf ein Sol-
daten, der als Untersuchungshäftling wegen eines vielleicht nur
geringen Deliktes eingeschlossen in der Zelle ohne Aussicht auf
rechtzeitige Hilfeleistung einen schweren Luftangriff über sich
ergehen lassen muss, darf in ihrer Bedeutung nicht unterschätzt
werden....

Bonhoeffer's memorandum on the occasion of an air raid warning

"What great words these still are. Why can I not simply
say what I mean, what I know? Or if I do not want to do
that, why not remain completely silent? How difficult it is
to do what is necessary and right without words, without
being understood."[91]

The dark tones of Bonhoeffer's written testimony from
Tegel are, however, never the expression of despair. Hitler,
the terrible fate that had gained the upper hand over him
and his friends, was to him already dead and no longer

139

worth a single line. At that time Bonhoeffer was far from letting himself be forced into an other-worldly attitude in his cell. In contrast to his feeling in 1933 or 1935 he did not allow himself to escape into apocalyptic longing, and this was part of the secret of his strength. In these extraordinary circumstances he reached maturity: "There are people who regard it as frivolous, and some Christians think it impious, for anyone to hope and prepare for a better earthly future. They think that the meaning of present events is chaos, disorder and catastrophe; and in resignation or pious escapism they surrender all responsibility for reconstruction and for future generations. It may be that the day of judgement will dawn tomorrow; in that case, we shall gladly stop working for a better future. But not before."[92]

9 *Works*

At first sight it would seem impossible to attempt a survey of Bonhoeffer's work as a whole; indeed, he has been criticized for its lack of unity. Nevertheless, it does provide us with detailed evidence of a consistent development and genuine message. At present there is a definite discrepancy between the world-wide references made to Bonhoeffer's work (and the many editions of his books) and the fact that very few professional theologians of any standing concern themselves with his ideas. What is the reason for this?

*

Dietrich Bonhoeffer had no opportunity to mature and perfect his life-work and it is a laborious task to reconstruct his ideas, after the event, from his books and collections of many of his essays, letters and notes. Some of these make light and stimulating reading, others are almost incomprehensible except to the specialist.

In addition it is not easy to determine his relationship to the great theologians who did leave behind them a life-work, and whose nearness to or distance from Bonhoeffer can be interpreted very differently. Bonhoeffer himself only rarely discussed them at any length.

It would, for instance, be interesting to know what Bonhoeffer really thought about the work of Karl Barth, to whom he was probably more indebted than to anyone else except Luther. He always approached him critically, however, especially towards the end as regards his "Revelation positivism", which should in fact be attributed less to Barth than to his followers. Bonhoeffer unfortunately knew only the four volumes then published out of the final thirteen volumes of Barth's great work *Church Dogmatics*.

Karl Barth, 1934

And it remains uncertain how his relationship would have developed to Rudolf Bultmann, with whose programme of de-mythologizing and "existential interpretation" of the New Testament Bonhoeffer's attempts have simply been mistakenly equated. He might also have changed his opinion of Paul Tillich, of whom he was critical, since he knew only his early work, published before Tillich's emigration in 1933.

It is difficult to decide whether he would have considered Tillich's universalism, his inspired study of the relevance of theological statements, as relevant to his own work, or whether he would have rejected him because of the "religiosity" of his interpretation of mankind and the world, in contrast to the "non-religious" interpretation Bonhoeffer himself favoured. In 1963, in his bestseller

142

Rudolf Bultmann

Honest to God,[93] John Robinson, then Bishop of Wool-wich, identified Bonhoeffer, in essentials, with Bultmann and Tillich. It is doubtful whether his description of Bonhoeffer's work really represents it adequately, but these references stimulated a new and world-wide interest both in Bonhoeffer as a phenomenon and in his work.

Dr Robinson's comments illustrate how initially only the scant fifty pages of theological discussion in the Tegel letters of 1944 bore fruit. It was precisely the frank, un-polished letter form of Bonhoeffer's last theological reflections which fascinated people, and which also misled them into making his formulations say what they wanted them to say, or else into developing his thought in such a way that a reading of Bonhoeffer as a whole could never support. Perhaps William Hamilton, the American "death of God" theologian, went too far when he answered a ques-

143

tion about whether he was justified in citing Bonhoeffer inaccurately, with the words: "Naturally, we make a creative misuse of Bonhoeffer." Yet his remark is not so very out of place. Bonhoeffer was, in fact, an inspired innovator. He would probably have asked in his turn: "Do you realize what you are setting in motion and how do you intend to justify it?", for he possessed a keen sense of tradition. In 1933 he wrote for his theological students: "Why should it be considered appropriate and even essential for a student of theology to speak dismissively of theological studies right from his first semester until he reaches the highest spiritual offices of the Church? Why should it be a particularly good sign for him to be averse to the company of honourable theologians from Paul to Augustine, Aquinas to Luther, to feel that it is unnecessary for him to have something that they considered of inestimable value? . . . Since when has the fact that he imitates popular opinion in his indifference to theology been a special recommendation for a theologian? And finally, since when has it been a qualification for the Christian to talk grandiosely about things of which he understands nothing?"[94]

Bonhoeffer's exploration of spheres totally at variance with this background of respect for tradition and his support for the progressive emancipation movement, which was taboo to his friends, caused him to be accused of inconsistency after the publication of the Tegel letters.

There are, however, more profound reasons for the reservations about Bonhoeffer's work evinced in theological faculties than his unfinished fragments and the letter form of his Tegel theology. They stem from the actual content of this theology and its connection with his life.

At no point is it possible to understand Bonhoeffer's theological work without reference to the actual here and now. His theology draws its vitality from the risks inherent in action. Bonhoeffer could communicate a surprising sense of presence: "What is true for always, is precisely not true for 'today'. God is 'always' God for us, in the sense that he is God 'today'."[95] Because of such views Bonhoeffer has been accused of lacking the "eschatological element" and of losing sight of the doctrine of the last things. Here lies one of the reasons for the difference between him and Karl Barth, whose theory of an "eschatological proviso" includes the idea of the non-presence of the beyond. A careful reading will show that this was by no means foreign to Bonhoeffer either. But he feared the temptation that it offered (not one, of course, that affected Barth himself), if the doctrine were distorted during the then Nazi period so that Christians could remain uninvolved in the challenges of the time.

With his concept of "today" Bonhoeffer retained an acute awareness of the dangers of hiding in the purely verbal, as represented by the Protestant doctrine of the "Word" of God. His fight against the watchword which had become a fetish, "by word alone", brought his work to the brink of heresy as far as the Lutheran tradition was concerned. Even today the Church feels challenged by Bonhoeffer's profoundly "politicized" understanding of the word. He is uncomfortably relevant, even at those points where his work adopts an apparently conservative form of language.

The "here and now" emphasis in Bonhoeffer's work is thus also closely connected with his life. These aspects of his personality reflect his consciousness of a problem with which the churches came only later to concern themselves, the problem of their power and lack of power, of their legitimate authority.

For Bonhoeffer this was also a personal problem. It underlies his entire work, even when he was putting forward abstract arguments, as he did in his early years. There is already an indication of it in the letter he wrote to Erwin Sutz at the time of the publication of his habilitation thesis, *Act and Being*, in 1931: "I have grown rather out of sympathy over the years with this my early product."[96] He feared that such "theologizing" was merely a manipulative game.

Clifford Green, an Australian theologian working in the

U.S.A., has shown conclusively[97] how Bonhoeffer in his book *The Cost of Discipleship*, tried to come to terms with the problem of his personal power by building up a super-powerful figure of Christ, who demanded total obedience; and how, especially in Tegel, he grew able to accept that he himself, with his own power and his own weakness, might be a source of strength for others. In the process, elements were added to his image of Christ which better reflected the mystery of Jesus of Nazareth: that is, he could be strong enough no longer to need constantly to assert himself, but could sacrifice himself whole-heartedly. In fact Bonhoeffer's realization in Tegel of his own capacity to be a liberating neighbour to his fellow-men flows over into his description of what the nature of a future Church should be. The concentration of earlier works, which could occasionally show signs of being forced, gives way to sure and confident writing.

If such biographical connections make Bonhoeffer's work particularly attractive, they do, none the less, also make it less easily classifiable according to other systems.

Bonhoeffer's total personal involvement is, sometimes unconsciously, a barrier and source of uneasiness for many of an older generation who have not thus involved themselves. They therefore reject the phenomenon as something alien to them, or refute it with standard theological excuses (the destruction of the theology of the word and the disintegration of the doctrine of the two kingdoms). Therefore in Germany many of the people who did not fight against the Third Reich are not interested in Bonhoeffer or are even hostile towards him, whereas he faces no such antagonism abroad. Wherever the churches are under pressure or have lost their freedom as institutions, Bonhoeffer's work is eagerly read and discussed. And this is especially so in places where groups have embarked upon experiments with new structures.

*

It is helpful to survey Bonhoeffer's work in the light of

Martin Luther, painting by Lucas Cranach the Elder, 1532

catchwords which epitomize the different stages of his theological development. *Christ existing as community* sums up the first, more academic phase of the books *Sanctorum Communio* and *Act and Being*. *Cheap and costly grace* stands for the next, more ecclesiastical phase of *The Cost of Discipleship* and *Life Together*. *The last things and the penultimate things* belongs to the period of *Ethics*. And finally *non-religious interpretation, a world come of age, Jesus the man for others*, and *the Church for others* belong to his time in Tegel, and are contained in *Letters and Papers from Prison*.

Bonhoeffer was a good stylist who coined memorable epigrammatic phrases, some of which are still current today, their authorship unsuspected by those who use them without much understanding of their intended meaning. The list quoted above betrays a trend away from the complicated towards the simple, but also from what is difficult to understand to what is almost too easily elucidated.

For Bonhoeffer these different stages were far from being leaps between opposite theses, for his central theological message always remained the same: Christ and his Church were his constant preoccupation. For him the Church gives substance to Christ and Christ corrects the Church. Bonhoeffer began with the pre-eminence of the Church and ended with the pre-eminence of the teaching of Christ. His modes of thinking and way of life altered, as did his companions and his audience, and they contributed to deepening the central message; they clarified his way of asking and answering.

So in 1933, in his University lecture, he put the question – as if there were one answer for all time – "Who is Christ?" It is worth noting that he was already asking "who" and not "what", that he was not looking for an object of study, but was rather willing to risk a personal encounter. In Tegel in 1944 he was searching for a "who" just as intensively but with one important qualification: "Who is Christ for us today?" He could only ask the question for himself and for his own time. The "us today" to whom he referred are, however, specific twofold heirs: firstly, heirs of a certain form of Christianity, a western way of thought and ecclesiastical organization that is centuries old and no longer has much in common with Christ's Biblical Gospel; and, secondly, heirs, and at all events beneficiaries, as believers or non-believers, of the Enlightenment with its emancipatory gains and losses. *Who is Christ for us today?* – for us who live with this dual heritage? – this finally became the vital question of his life. This is why, at the end, his theological thought had an astounding breadth. All his life Feuerbach's questioning rang in his ears: "Feuerbach presented theology with two questions which it has not answered: the question of whether its statements are true and the question of its correspondence to life."[98] The heart-felt desire to meet Christ in truth and in reality lies behind all Bonhoeffer's work from the beginning to the end.

*

The first formula, *Christ existing as community*, he coined in his dissertation in 1925, and it remained alive in his theology until the early thirties. It modified Hegel's concept of "God existing as community". Hegel meant by this the dwelling of the Holy Spirit as absolute spirit in the community. Bonhoeffer turned the formula into a christological one.

Inspired by his experience of Rome, he discovered the phenomenon of the Church. Where can salvation be found on the earth? In the social model of a community gathered together through and in Christ. There his presence and his gifts are met in living form. The Church is as much a theological as a sociological entity. In it the God *extra nos* (outside us) shows himself to be *pro nobis* (for us). So Bonhoeffer wrote a "dogmatic enquiry into the sociology of the Church" (subtitle); "the congregation of the faithful remains our Mother."[99]

Thus, right from the beginning, what interested Bonhoeffer was not so much metaphysical speculation about the hereafter nor transcendental notions of the divine Idea, but the self-binding relationship of God with the living physical community of Christ. He was interested not by itemized experiences of piety but by the bond with this tangible, constant dimension of the gathered congregation.

Long after Bonhoeffer's death Barth wrote: "I openly confess that I have misgivings whether I can even maintain [i.e. in my ecclesiology] the high level reached by Bonhoeffer, saying no less in my own words and context, and saying it no less forcefully, than did this young man so many years ago."[100]

In *Act and Being*, his habilitation thesis written in 1931, Bonhoeffer conducted a competent analysis of dialectical theology, including Bultmann and, in particular, the early Heidegger (*Being and Time*). Here too his strong desire to emphasise the real accessibility of God to man is evident: "In Revelation it is a question less of God's freedom on the far side from us, i.e. his eternal isolation and aseity, than of his forth-proceedings in this revelation, his *given* Word, his bond in which he has bound himself, of his freedom as it is most strongly attested in his having freely bound himself to historical man, having placed himself at man's disposal. God is not free *of* man but *for* man. Christ is the word of his freedom. God *is there*, which is to say: not in eternal non-objectivity but (looking ahead for the moment) 'haveable', graspable in his word within the Church."[101] The specialist will recognize the extent of the theologically and historically based reservations and attacks, including those against Barth's Calvinism.

*

Cheap grace and costly grace was a phrase which soon spread far beyond specialist theological circles. It appeared first in *The Cost of Discipleship*, the first drafts of which go back to 1931–32 and which was published in 1937. The formula arose from his reading of Kierkegaard.

Behind the phrase lies Bonhoeffer's position as a public preacher, lecturer, and officially active ecumenist. He felt it his responsibility that words were addressed to the world and the churches which bore no relation in importance and efficacy to what they meant. How could it be tolerated that the Church and the preacher too should use the most valuable gift of all, the word of the nearby God himself, so ineffectively?

The book is therefore highly critical of the Church. The discrepancy between its mandate to preach publicly the Word and its noticeable lack of voice led Bonhoeffer to the problem of its authorization, its credibility, and from there to an examination and renewal of the profession of its preachers.

He sought the answer not in a renewal of the doctrine of the office of the ministry but in a way of life which could re-establish the importance of the word: the renewal of authority and credibility through discipleship alone. This was not intended to imply any shift in emphasis from faith to works or to an ethic of the ministry, but on the contrary a new re-instatement of the *sola gratia*, by grace alone, of the Reformation. So he wrote:

"Cheap grace is the deadly enemy of our Church. We are fighting today for costly grace.

"Cheap grace means grace sold on the market like cheapjack's wares. The sacraments, the forgiveness of sins, and the consolations of religion are thrown away at cut prices. Grace is represented as the Church's inexhaustible treasury, from which it showers blessings with generous hands, without asking questions or fixing limits. Grace without price; grace without cost . . .

"Cheap grace means grace as a doctrine, a principle, a system . . . In such a Church the world finds a cheap covering for its sins; no contrition is required, still less any real desire to be delivered from sin. Cheap grace therefore amounts to a denial of the living Word of God, in fact, a denial of the Incarnation of the Word of God.

"Cheap grace means the justification of sin and not the justification of the sinner. Grace alone does everything, they say, and so everything can remain as it was before . . . Cheap grace is the grace we bestow on ourselves . . . Cheap grace is grace without discipleship, grace without the cross, grace without Jesus Christ, living and incarnate."

Luther, in Bonhoeffer's view, was concerned with this costly grace, "not the justification of sin, but the justification of the sinner . . . Yet the outcome of the Reformation

Eberhard Bethge

was the victory, not of Luther's perception of grace in all its purity and costliness, but of the vigilant religious instinct of man for the place where grace is to be obtained at the cheapest price. All that was needed was a subtle and almost imperceptible change of emphasis, and the damage was done. . . . When he spoke of grace, Luther always implied as a corollary that it cost him his own life, the life which was now for the first time subjected to the absolute obedience of Christ . . . Luther had said that grace alone can save; his followers took up his doctrine and repeated it literally. But they left out its invariable corollary, the obligation of discipleship. There was no need for Luther always to mention that corollary explicitly, for he always spoke as one who had been led by grace to the strictest following of Christ. Judged by the standard of Luther's doctrine, that of his followers was unassailable, and yet their orthodoxy spelt the end and destruction of the Reformation as the revelation on earth of the costly grace of God."

There is one particularly relevant sentence here which can be seen as a key to Bonhoeffer's thought: "This means that a perception cannot be separated from the existence in which it is gained."

He made a shrewd analysis of the state of the Church: "We Lutherans have gathered like eagles round the carcase of cheap grace, and there we have drunk of the poison which has killed the life of following Christ. It is true, of course, that we have paid the doctrine of pure grace divine honours unparalleled in Christendom, in fact we have exalted that doctrine to the position of God himself. Everywhere Luther's formula has been repeated, but its truth perverted into self-deception. So long as our Church holds the correct doctrine of justification, there is no doubt whatever that it is a justified Church ... The result was that a nation became Christian and Lutheran, but at the cost of true discipleship. The price it was called upon to pay was all too cheap. Cheap grace had won the day ... The price we are having to pay today in the shape of the collapse of the organized Church is only the inevitable consequence of our policy of making grace available to all at too low a cost ... This cheap grace has been no less disastrous to our own spiritual lives. Instead of opening up the way to Christ, it has closed it ... The word of cheap grace has been the ruin of more Christians than any commandment of works."

Many of the great men of the Protestant tradition, like Luther and Barth, have made their reputation with a commentary on the Epistle to the Romans; Bonhoeffer made himself known to a wider circle with an exegesis of the Sermon on the Mount which followed the early passages quoted above.

Some people have seen the danger in Bonhoeffer's theology of the discipleship of Christians creating a Christian ghetto for themselves. The now famous key concept in the book: "Only he who believes is obedient, and only he who is obedient believes"[102], aroused little positive enthusiasm for its equation of faith and obedience. Was he perhaps making too many demands, instead of creating an area of freedom?

It is noticeable that before 1933 Bonhoeffer achieved a breadth of themes and of relevance to the world, which then diminished and did not reappear until the period of *Ethics* and the Tegel letters. In January 1935 he wrote to his brother Karl-Friedrich on his birthday: "I think I know that I will really only be truly clear and honest when I really come to terms in all seriousness, with the Sermon on the Mount. Here is the only source of power which could blow the whole glamour and glitter sky-high [he is referring to the Nazi Reich here] until only a few burnt-out remains are left of the fireworks. The renewal of the Church will certainly come from a new type of monasticism, which has in common with the old only the uncompromising nature of a life lived according to the Sermon on the Mount as a disciple of Christ. I believe it is high time for men to band together to do this."[103]

So Dietrich Bonhoeffer believes that theology and preaching would only emerge from their pointless busy activity if the Church lived, interpreted and demanded its faith as discipleship, liberating for a new life, independent of other authorities.

During the years of its composition *The Cost of Discipleship* was anything but a retreat into a ghetto. On the contrary, it was a firm rejection of conformity, of homogenization, an attack on the current National Socialist religion. At the same time *The Cost of Discipleship* attacked the mild and neutral compromises with this religion made by the so-called Reformed theologians.

The time came, however, when even preaching discipleship became sterile and pointless. In his first letter after the *putsch* failed, on 21 July 1944, Bonhoeffer described how he had come to the end of a path passionately pursued with his book on *The Cost of Discipleship*: "I suppose I wrote *The Cost of Discipleship* as the end of that path [that is, the attempt 'to live a holy life or something like it']. Today I can see the dangers of that book, though I still stand by what I wrote."[104]

He did not go back on the concept of grace as costly

rather than cheap; indeed, to hold to grace had become even more costly in 1944 than it had seemed in 1935. This is why he maintains: "I still stand by what I wrote."

*

The best-known phrase in his book *Ethics* has been *the ultimate things and the penultimate things.* The book was not planned by Bonhoeffer in the form in which we have it today. It contains the posthumous collection of at least four unfinished essays, each one begun anew by Bonhoeffer during the years from 1939 to 1943. A supplement offers further essays and pieces of work on the subject of ethics, all dating from the same period. Among them is the particularly attractive, although unfortunately unfinished study entitled *What is meant by telling the truth?*[105] which Bonhoeffer drafted in Tegel during the cross-examinations with all their camouflages and lies. After the editor's initial attempt to arrange the different sections of *Ethics* systematically according to an old plan of Bonhoeffer's (the first to fifth editions), the passages have now been grouped chronologically, as they were written.

It is clear, looking at it today, how Bonhoeffer's thinking gained in depth during this period of journeys (on behalf of the *Abwehr*) and peaceful weeks in Ettal and Pomerania. *Ethics* begins much in the same style as *The Cost of Discipleship*, and ends in a style very reminiscent of the Tegel letters.

The repeated new beginnings characteristic of *Ethics* provide a glimpse, as it were, of the workshop rather than the final display. The fragments which form the book are characterized by a determined and sustained effort to bring out fully the relatedness of Christ and consequently the relatedness to the world: "Everything would be ruined if one were to try to reserve Christ for the Church and to allow the world only some kind of law, even if it were a Christian law. Christ died for the world, and *it is only in the midst of the world that Christ is Christ.*"[106]

It is only in the midst of the world that Christ is Christ is a strong statement and Bonhoeffer goes on to justify it as follows: in Christ's Incarnation man and the world are in the process of acceptance, in Christ's Cross they are in the process of being judged and reconciled, and in Christ's Resurrection they are in the process of the renewal of life. In 1932 the actual world for Bonhoeffer was a sphere in which he had to preach the Word and which he had to integrate into the Church. In 1935 the world became the dark valley in which there should be no delay, no tarrying. Now the world becomes a partner. Bonhoeffer's relationship to reality becomes strikingly more positive. There can be no reality without Christ and no Christ without reality. This means that Christ is not an absolute norm, which is super-imposed on reality from outside, and reality is not a mere vehicle on which Christian ethical philosophers can imprint their programmes. Christ does not cancel out reality but brings it to fulfilment through judgement, atonement and renewal. He does not make it "Christian". The good in and for the world is no abstract idea, but a constant process which consists of accepting human beings and taking part fully in life. Ethics, according to Bonhoeffer, "is learning to live together. The commandment of Christ frees the created to the fulfilment of its inherent law", the cross of atonement "is the setting free for life in genuine worldliness"; it means "that men are there who stand as deputies for the other men, for the whole world."[107]

The most illuminating formula to express this central relatedness of Christ and the world, so that they do not merely mutually cancel out or sanction one another but remain what they are, neither deduced nor derived, is that concept of *the ultimate and the penultimate things*. The last word, Christ, (Bonhoeffer can also say: the last word of "justification") is ungraspable; it embraces both the beginning and the end as the penultimate, whether these are thought of temporally, spatially or qualitatively. The last things define the penultimate things and give them validity as well as power. So Christ "neither renders the human reality independent nor destroys it, but he allows

156

it to remain as that which is before the last, as a penultimate which requires to be taken seriously in its own right,
and yet not to be taken seriously ... Christian life means
neither a destruction nor a sanctioning of the penultimate
... it is participation in the encounter of Christ with
the world."[108]

Because of this dynamic synopsis of Christ's reality and
of actual world structures, many people think that, in spite
of its incomplete condition, *Ethics* is Bonhoeffer's most
profound and important work. In fact he overcame in one
leap the old classic conflict in ethics: that between a norm
ethic and a situation ethic; that is to say, he was aware of
the advantages of both and avoided the disadvantages. A
norm ethic provides for the continuity of ethical decisions,
but it ends in remoteness from the world, distorts reality
with all-embracing casuistry; it ignores Christ's Incarnation and its closeness to life. During the Nazi period it had
certain qualities of endurance to offer, but it remained sterile and failed in the real historical situation. A situation
ethic, on the other hand, provides for the closeness of reality, but causes the disintegration of the whole in day-to-
day individual decisions, and it remains questionable
whether it can really make a helpful contribution to what
is historically relevant and necessary. It is dangerously
near the mere sanctioning of the *status quo*; it misses
Christ's cross and its vital power.

Ethical systems which are close to reality today rapidly
become obsolete. Parts of Bonhoeffer's ethic are no excep-
tion. A vast number of areas of life, which are scarcely or
unsatisfactorily dealt with in Bonhoeffer's work, have
gained a new perspective in the intervening years because
of advances in psychology, sociology, the human sciences,
cybernetics and experimental techniques, and have thrown
complicated problems into relief. Certain sections, such as
those containing comments on the State and society, seem
in the light of present-day problems of the redistribution
of power like documents of bygone conservatism.

None the less, the Lutheran Bonhoeffer broke through

the walls of the Lutheran doctrine of the two kingdoms, which were becoming ever higher and have still not been dismantled even today. By suggesting a so-called doctrine of the mandate in ethics he resolved the problem of the static philosophy of two estates and two pillars (the State and the Church as God's only mandates in the world). He attacked the sterile thinking in terms of two kingdoms, of which he says: "... the main underlying conception in ethical thought, and the one which consciously or unconsciously has determined its whole course, has been the conception of a juxtaposition and conflict of two spheres, the one divine, holy, supernatural and Christian, and the other worldly, profane, natural and un-Christian."[109] In this way he outlined clearly the tasks facing an ethic for today and pointed out elements for a solution to the problem.

*

The phrases *non-religious interpretation, the world's coming of age, the man for others, the Church for others* all come from those fifty pages of letters from prison, which were written between 30 April and 23 August 1944.

One or two side comments in the middle of his work on *Ethics*, occasioned by the encounters in those last years and his intensive reading in his prison cell, show that Bonhoeffer intended to write a short book on the situation of Christianity in the modern world. It was never written. All we have is correspondence on this subject and a short summary of the plan for the book (Outline for a Book[110]). He probably wrote a good deal on the subject after 23 August in Tegel, and even in Prinz-Albrecht-Strasse. This was the only manuscript that he did not give his father to take home. He kept it with him because he was still working on it, and it was lost at the time of his last journey, to death.

The letters and drafts which have been preserved are addressed to his friend and fellow-theologian. This means that the reflections are not all substantiated, but are partly in shorthand for someone who shared with him the same ideas, the same conceptual background and the same theological world. The concept of "religion", for example, was naturally understood by both of them in the tradition of Luther (religion comes from the flesh, faith from the spirit) and in the same sense as the Barthian critique of religion, which makes a strong distinction between faith and religion. The fact that many readers of *Letters and Papers from Prison* did not share these assumptions led to the misapprehension that in his critical attitude to religion Bonhoeffer intended to discard prayer and piety too.

Non-religious interpretation as a concept comes, therefore, from this world of theologians critical of religion and naturally also from an interest in exegesis – although far more lies behind it. The idea of the world coming of age sprang from his fresh intensive reading of Dilthey during the winter of 1943–44, as well as from his earlier knowledge of Kant (the Enlightenment as "man's emergence from a self-imposed minority . . .") *Jesus, the man for others* and *the Church for others* had long been ideas in the mainstream of Bonhoeffer's thought. He first wanted to express the Reformers' *pro me* (for me) of the Gospel as the plural *pro nobis* (for us) and then gradually came to insist that even the *pro nobis* should be transformed into *pro aliis* (for others). At all events the simple and yet profoundly felt "for others" only came to fruition in the last stages of writing *Ethics*, and then in *Outline for a Book*, written in Tegel. It offers the most concise answer to Bonhoeffer's most vital question: "Who is Christ for us today?"

The explicit expression of his Tegel theology began with the famous letter of 30 April 1944. After Bonhoeffer had assured his friend that, after all the worry over the postponement of the date for the trial he was in good health, he continued:

"You would be surprised, and perhaps even worried, by my theological thoughts and the conclusions that they lead to . . . What is bothering me incessantly is the question what Christianity really is, or indeed who Christ really is,

159

for us today. The time when people could be told every-thing by means of words, whether theological or pious, is over, and so is the time of inwardness and conscience – and that means the time of religion in general. We are moving towards a completely religionless time; people as they are now simply cannot be religious any more. . . . It means that the foundation is taken away from the whole of what has up to now been our 'Christianity', and that there remain only a few 'last survivors of the age of chiv-alry', or a few intellectually dishonest people, on whom we can descend as 'religious' . . . Are we to fall upon a few unfortunate people in their hour of need and exercise a sort of religious compulsion on them? If we don't want to do all that, if our final judgement must be that the western form of Christianity, too, was only a preliminary stage to a complete absence of religion, what kind of situation emerges for us, for the Church? How can Christ become the Lord of the religionless as well? Are there religionless Christians? If religion is only a garment of Christianity – and even this garment has looked very different at differ-ent times – then what is a religionless Christianity? . . .

"The questions to be answered would surely be: What do a church, a community, a sermon, a liturgy, a Christian life mean in a religionless world? How do we speak of God – without religion, i.e. without the temporally conditioned presuppositions of metaphysics, inwardness, and so on? How do we speak (or perhaps we cannot now even 'speak' as we used to) in a 'secular' way about 'God'? In what way are we 'religionless-secular' Christians, in what way are we the *ekklesia*, those who are called forth, not regarding our-selves from a religious point of view as specially favoured, but rather as belonging wholly to the world? In that case Christ is no longer an object of religion, but something quite different, really the Lord of the world . . .

"Religious people speak of God when human knowledge . . . has come to an end, or when human resources fail – in fact it is always the *deus ex machina* that they bring on to the scene, either for the apparent solution of insoluble prob-

lems, or as strength in human failure – always, that is to
say, exploiting human weakness or human boundaries . . .
I should like to speak of God not on the boundaries but at
the centre, not in weaknesses but in strength; and therefore
not in death and guilt but in man's life and goodness. As
to the boundaries, it seems to me better to be silent and
leave the insoluble unsolved. Belief in the resurrection is
not the 'solution' of the problem of death. God's 'beyond'
is not the beyond of our cognitive faculties. The transcendence of epistemological theory has nothing to do with the
transcendence of God. God is beyond in the midst of our
life."[111]

It is clear that what Bonhoeffer is undertaking here goes
far beyond interpretation and is an attempt to formulate a
new "religionless Christianity".

As a sort of postscript to this wide-ranging first letter
there followed on 5 May the initially more limited question: "What does it mean to 'interpret in a religious
sense'?" The question is put in order to establish what a
non-religious interpretation might mean. Bonhoeffer's
answer is: "I think it means to speak on the one hand
metaphysically, and on the other hand individualistically.
Neither of these is relevant to the Biblical message or to
the man of today."[112]

The Biblical Gospel is, therefore, not to be equated with
the Christian edifice of dogmas, which the early and
medieval Church turned it into with the tools of its philosophical conceptions and language (this is what Bonhoeffer
means by "metaphysics"). Man today no longer thinks
"metaphysically" like this. Nor is the Biblical Gospel to be
equated with the individual's quest for the merciful God.
In his first letter Bonhoeffer named two elements which
would need to be overcome in any non-religious interpretation of the message, because they had corrupted this
message: these were, the rights and privileges which had
made the Church play the role of a sovereign with depend-
ants.

Here Bonhoeffer's non-religious interpretation clearly

moves far beyond the plane of purely interpretative problems. It concerns the form of the Church. "Religionless Christianity" is accordingly first and foremost a self-critical penitential act on the part of the Church which cannot be fulfilled at the writing-desk. Therefore Bonhoeffer says: "We are once again being driven right back to the beginnings of our understanding... Our church, which has been fighting in these years only for its self-preservation, as though that were an end in itself, is incapable of taking the word of reconciliation and redemption to mankind and the world. Our earlier words are therefore bound to lose their force and cease, and our being Christians today will be limited to two things: prayer and righteous action among men ... We are not yet out of the melting-pot [of the church's form], and any attempt to help the church prematurely to a new expansion of its organization will merely delay its conversion and purification. It is not for us to prophesy the day (though the day will come) when men will once more be called so to utter the word of God that the world will be changed and renewed by it. It will be a new language, perhaps quite non-religious, but liberating and redeeming – as was Jesus' language; it will shock people and yet overcome them by its power; it will be the language of a new righteousness and truth, proclaiming God's peace with men and the coming of his kingdom ... Till then the Christian cause will be a silent and hidden affair, but there will be those who pray and do right and wait for God's own time."[113]

At the beginning of June 1944 there emerged a complementary concept to that of the non-religious interpretation: Christ and "the world that has come of age". In the intervening period Bonhoeffer had described how the world had rejected a stopgap God and discovered its own autonomy in all areas of life, in contrast with its medieval dependency on the Church. Until then the Church had seen this development towards and during the Enlightenment only as an apostasy. Now the writer depicts this irreligion and autonomy, which had arisen in opposition to

162

the Church, in a positive sense as the world's coming of age: "Efforts are made [by the Church's apologists] to prove to a world thus come of age that it cannot live without the tutelage of 'God' . . . The attack by Christian apologetics on the adulthood of the world I consider to be in the first place pointless, in the second place ignoble, and in the third place unchristian. Pointless, because it seems to me like an attempt to put a grown-up man back into adolescence, i.e. to make him dependent on things on which he is, in fact, no longer dependent, and thrusting him into problems that are, in fact, no longer problems to him. Ignoble, because it amounts to an attempt to exploit man's weakness for purposes that are alien to him and to which he has not freely assented. Unchristian, because it confuses Christ with one particular stage in man's religiousness, i.e. with a human law . . . The question is: Christ and the world that has come of age."[114]

And again one month later, after renewed criticism of ecclesiastical attacks on the world's adulthood and of the churches' specialization in the "secrets known to a man's valet", Bonhoeffer wrote: "I therefore want to start from the premise that God shouldn't be smuggled into some last secret place, but that we should frankly recognize that the world, and people, have come of age, that we shouldn't run man down in his worldliness, but confront him with God at his strongest point [how autobiographical that is!], that we should give up all clerical tricks . . ."[115]

Until this point he had placed the main emphasis on an historico-philosophical and theologico-historical analysis in his description of Christianity. Now, as a theologian, he is concerned with a deeper understanding of Christ as an event in the world: Who *is he* for us today? After constant new demarcations Bonhoeffer eventually, in a letter of 16 July, arrived at an analysis which sums up almost too briefly and concentratedly the christological element:

"And we cannot be honest unless we recognize that we have to live in the world *etsi deus non daretur*. And this is just what we do recognize – before God! God himself compels us to recognize it. So our coming of age leads us to a true recognition of our situation before God. God would have us know that we must live as men who manage our lives without him. The God who is with us is the God who forsakes us (Mark 15:34: "My God, my God, why hast thou forsaken me?") The God who lets us live in the world without the working hypothesis of God is the God before whom we stand continually. Before God and with God we live without God. God lets himself be pushed out of the world on to the cross. He is weak and powerless in the world, and that is precisely the way, the only way, in which he is with us and helps us. Matthew 8:17 ("This was to fulfil what was spoken by the prophet Isaiah, 'He took our infirmities and bore our diseases'.") makes it quite clear that Christ helps us, not by virtue of his omnipotence, but by virtue of his weakness and suffering.

"Here is the decisive difference between Christianity and all other religions. Man's religiosity makes him look in his distress to the power of God in the world: God is the *deus ex machina*. The Bible directs man to God's powerlessness and suffering; only the suffering God can help. To that extent we may say that the development towards the world's coming of age outlined above, which has done away with a false conception of God, opens up a way of seeing the God of the Bible, who wins power and space in the world by his weakness. This will probably be the starting-point for our 'secular interpretation'."[116]

This central core to Bonhoeffer's work is, of course, present earlier, especially in *The Cost of Discipleship*. And it has a biographical element. When his niece Marianne Leibholz was confirmed after the family had emigrated, he wrote from Switzerland to his sister Sabine in Oxford (21 May 1942): "It is a good thing to learn early that God and suffering are not opposites but rather one and the same thing and necessarily so; for me the idea that God himself suffers is far and away the most convincing piece of Christian doctrine."[117]

164

What does this *theologia crucis* mean for man? What makes a man a Christian? In contrast to the "religious" man, the Christian learns the "reversal of what the religious man expects from God. Man is summoned to share in God's sufferings at the hand of a godless world. He must therefore really live in the godless world, without attempting to gloss over or explain its ungodliness in some religious way or other. He must live a 'secular' life, and thereby share in God's suffering. He *may* live a 'secular' life (as one who has been freed from false religious obligations and inhibitions). To be a Christian does not mean to be religious in a particular way, to make something of oneself (a sinner, a penitent, or a saint) on the basis of some method or other, but to be a man – not a type of man, but the man that Christ creates in us. It is not the religious act that makes the Christian, but participation in the sufferings of God in the secular life. That is *metanoia*: not in the first place thinking about one's own needs, problems, sins, and fears, but allowing oneself to be caught up into the way of Jesus Christ, into the messianic event, thus fulfilling Isaiah 53 . . .

"The 'religious act' is always something partial; 'faith' is something whole, involving the whole of one's life. Jesus calls men, not to a new religion, but to life. But what does this life look like, this participation in the powerlessness of God in the world? I will write about that next time, I hope."[118]

Before he could write again, however, the *putsch* had failed. Perhaps the details of "what this life looks like" have been set out in the letter he wrote on 21 July 1944, which has already been quoted. Or perhaps the way that Bonhoeffer's own life ended and the circumstances of his death, were the continuation of what is adumbrated here, and so more vividly represented than they could be by any pen.

After 20 July, however, there was another postponement. And in the interim Bonhoeffer sent off the *Outline for a Book*. It puts forward a synopsis of the three chapters

Bonhoeffer intended to write: (1) A Stocktaking of Christianity, (2) The Real Meaning of Christian Faith, (3) Conclusions.[119]

In this summary it is again clear how Bonhoeffer had been stimulated and disturbed by that argument of Feuerbach and of Marxism which claims that theology is only anthropology, religion an expression of promises of the fulfilment in another world of man's desires in this world, and Christianity consequently only a sublimation of human needs. Bonhoeffer reverses this thesis. For Feuerbach man subjects himself to an almighty God; his aim is to turn the servants of a despotic God into atheists, "the candidates for the next world into students of this world". In the Christian, Biblical experience of God Bonhoeffer sees the opposite: it is not man who subjects himself to an almighty God, but God who subjects himself to mankind in the frailty of his suffering. The almighty *deus ex machina* of religions is for Bonhoeffer as for Feuerbach "a partial extension of the world". According to his concept this is only "religion". But "the encounter with Jesus Christ" is "the experience that an inversion of all human life is given in the fact that 'Jesus is there only for others'. His 'being there for others' is the experience of transcendence. It is only this 'being there for others', maintained till death, that is the ground of his omnipotence, omniscience, and omnipresence. Faith is participation in this being of Jesus ... Our relation to God is not a 'religious' relationship to the highest, most powerful, and best Being imaginable – that is not authentic transcendence – but our relation to God is a new life in 'existence for others', through participation in the being of Jesus. The transcendental is not infinite and unattainable tasks, but the neighbour who is within reach in any given situation. God in human form – not, as in oriental religions, in animal form, monstrous, chaotic, remote, and terrifying, nor in the conceptual forms of the absolute, metaphysical, infinite, etc., nor yet in the Greek divine-human form of 'man in himself', but 'the man for others', and therefore the Crucified."[120]

For Bonhoeffer these thoughts mean that the Church, which he saw as irredeemably compromised by National Socialism, had to change itself radically: "To make a start, it should give away all its property to those in need. The clergy must live solely on the free-will offerings of their congregations, or possibly engage in some secular calling. The church must share in the secular problems of ordinary human life, not dominating, but helping and serving. It must tell men of every calling what it means to live in Christ, to exist for others . . . It is not abstract argument, but example, that gives its word emphasis and power."[121]

Dietrich Bonhoeffer was not able to visualize to himself the restoration that his church was to undergo after 1945. His suggestions must inevitably seem naïve to this re-established church. Nevertheless everyone can sense that he was not far from the truth and that the reality might some day be like this – as it is, for example, in Taizé now.

Bonhoeffer's view of religion as transient was of course attacked violently. But the fact that he was practising modern religious criticism remains just as important as the distinction between religion and "religion". Bonhoeffer's "religion" ought to stand permanently against that sort of religion which is simply self-aggrandizement at the expense of others.

There has also been criticism that what Bonhoeffer said implied the destruction of worship, piety and liturgy. It is true that he sees that this period, during which man's relationship with Christ has been compromised, makes a retreat into seclusion necessary: a retreat to *the secret discipline*:[122] (a term and practice of the early Church); but not so that faith is destroyed, rather so that it is possible to experience and communicate it again. Until then it is a question of "prayer and doing justly among men".

Criticism has also been directed against his thesis of the Church's and man's coming of age. The complaint here is that it cancels out the relationship between Christ and faith. But it is precisely man's relationship with Christ which requires him to encourage and ensure his neighbour's coming of age. For Bonhoeffer, to deny man's majority is to sin, whereas to ensure its preservation is not. What man who refuses this coming of age can truly justify his stand by reference to Christ?

Bonhoeffer expressed in a poem the theological thoughts which filled his mind in these last months. It is dated July 1944 and entitled *Christians and Pagans*[123]:

> Men go to God when they are sore bestead,
> Pray to him for succour, for his peace, for bread,
> For mercy for them sick, sinning, or dead;
> All men do so, Christian and unbelieving.

> Men go to God when he is sore bestead,
> Find him poor and scorned, without shelter or bread,
> Whelmed under weight of the wicked, the weak, the dead;
> Christians stand by God in his hour of grieving.

> God goes to every man when sore bestead,
> Feeds body and spirit with his bread;
> For Christians, pagans alike he hangs dead,
> And both alike forgiving.

The theological theme "Who is Christ for us today?" and the Christological answer "Jesus, the man for others" are expressed in three different forms in Bonhoeffer's life. A new form appears at each point when the old form can no longer cope with new historical challenges.

First of all, it was the cause of peace against nationalistic militarism; then, the fight against anti-Semitic racism; finally, the "being below" of the Church. Each stage meant he had to question his church's way of existence anew; finding an answer became each time more precarious. Each new step was unpopular and threatening – as it still is today.

The part Bonhoeffer played in the struggle for peace made him, a follower of Christ, an ally of the few pacifists, who were then very unpopular.

His resistance to Nazi racism – which could no longer be countered by a pacificist sermon on peace, because a sermon could not prevent complicity in murder – turned the preacher of peace into an ally of conspirators plotting to rid their country of the murderers.

In his own painful process of learning Bonhoeffer discovered the vision of a transformation process for Christianity: the liberation of his own church through a return to poverty, through a rejection of the position of hierarchical dominance which has developed theologically as well as historically, legally and economically, through a return down to Christ's way among men. Bonhoeffer seems to have had a premonition of the extent to which the ethic of our bond with the disadvantaged of this world would become a controversial subject in modern Christianity.

Notes

Bonhoeffer's general writings have been published in German as *Gesammelte Schriften I–VI*, referred to as GS. Extracts from these volumes have been translated into English and appear in:

No Rusty Swords, Collins, London and Harper & Row, New York, 1965

The Way to Freedom, Collins, London and Harper & Row, New York, 1966

True Patriotism, Collins, London and Harper & Row, New York, 1973

Christology, Collins, London and as *Christ the Center*, Harper & Row, New York, 1966. A new translation was published by both companies in paperback in 1978

1. GS II, Munich 1959, p. 441
2. James Mark, "Bonhoeffer reconsidered", in *Theology*, November 1973, p. 586
3. *Letters and Papers from Prison*, Enlarged Edition, SCM Press, London, and Macmillan, New York, 1971, p. 219
4. Ibid., p. 347f.
5. In *Deutsche Zeitschrift für Nervenheilkunde*, Vol. 161, p. 5f.
6. *Letters and Papers from Prison*, p. 386f.
7. J. Zutt, E. Strauss and H. Scheller (ed.): *K. Bonhoeffer zum 100. Geburtstag*, Berlin, 1969, p. 87
8. Eberhard Bethge, *Dietrich Bonhoeffer: Theologian–Christian–Contemporary*, Collins, London, 1970, and *Dietrich Bonhoeffer: Man of Vision – Man of Courage*, Harper & Row, New York, 1970. Both companies later published this volume in paperback (1977)
9. Zutt, Strauss and Scheller, *op. cit.*, p. 91
10. GS, *op. cit.*, p. 23f.
11. See Eberhard Bethge and Ronald C. Jasper (ed.): *An der Schwelle zum gespaltenen Europa*, Stuttgart, 1974
12. *Letters and Papers from Prison*, p. 77f.
13. Friedrich Naumann, *Briefe über Religion*, Berlin, 1917, p. 61
14. GS VI, Munich, 1974, p. 35
15. Ibid., p. 27
16. Ibid., p. 37f.
17. Ibid., p. 42
18. "The Church and the Proletariat", in *Sanctorum Communio*, Collins, London, and as *The Communion of Saints*, Harper & Row, New York, 1963

19. *Letters and Papers from Prison*, p. 129
20. GS, *op. cit.*, pp. 132, 105, 129, 168
21. GS III, Munich, 1960, pp. 62–84
22. Erik Peterson: *Theologische Traktate*, 1951, p. 301
23. Quotations in this section from GS I, Munich, 1958, p. 54; GS VI, p. 367; GS I, p. 54
24. GS I, Munich, 1958, p. 24
25. See GS VI, p. 203f.
26. GS II, p. 41
27. In *Hamburger Nachrichten* of 1 June 1931
28. GS I, pp. 18, 118
29. Ibid., p. 145
30. Ibid., p. 155
31. Ibid., pp. 155, 24, 35f.
32. GS VI, pp. 216, 218
33. GS I, pp. 25–8
34. GS IV, Munich, 1962, pp. 66, 94
35. 19 June 1932; quoted in GS IV, p. 71
36. *Letters and Papers from Prison*, p. 275f.
37. GS VI, p. 367f.
38. See GS II, pp. 19–38
39. Ibid., pp. 35, 37
40. GS I, p. 38
41. In *Der Vormarsch*; quoted in GS II, pp. 44–53
42. GS II, p. 48
43. Ibid., pp. 90–119
44. Both letters in GS II, pp. 130–7
45. Unpublished letter from Karl Bonhoeffer, 22 December 1933
46. GS II, p. 157
47. Gerhard Niemöller, *Die este Bekenntnissynode der DEK zu Barmen*, Göttingen, 1959, Vol. II, p. 56
48. GS VI, p. 350f.
49. GS I, p. 187
50. Ibid., pp. 216, 218f.
51. Ibid., pp. 40, 42f.
52. GS II, p. 458
53. Ibid., p. 284f.
54. Ibid., pp. 538, 344
55. Ibid., p. 238; cp. ibid., pp. 217–63, as well as GS VI, pp. 401–14
56. GS I, p. 42
57. GS II, pp. 308–15
58. See e.g. J. Beckmann, *Kirchliches Jahrbuch 1933–1944*, Gütersloh, 1948, pp. 351–6
59. GS I, p. 281f.
60. Ibid., pp. 297, 302f., 304–6, 320, 314f.
61. GS VI, pp. 531–4

62. GS I, pp. 355–71
63. GS II, pp. 640–3
64. See GS VI, pp. 581, 635–7
65. *Letters and Papers from Prison*, p. 174
66. GS II, p. 420
67. *Ethics*, SCM Press, London, 1971, p. 54
68. Ibid., p. 92
69. Ibid., pp. 208, 210
70. Quoted in *Letters and Papers from Prison*, pp. 3–17
71. Ibid., pp. 5f.,8f., 17
72. Ibid., p. 35
73. Ibid., pp. 249, 342
74. Ibid., pp. 56, 61
75. Ibid., pp. 56–69
76. Ibid., p. 60
77. Ibid., pp. 121–5
78. Ibid., p. 160f.
79. Ibid., p. 370f.
80. See Bethge, *op. cit.*, p. 664n. Also GS VI, p. 590f.
81. Hugh Falconer to Gerhard Leibholz on 1 October 1945; quoted in Bethge, *op. cit.*, p. 826
82. GS I, p. 412
83. See Bernadette Morand, *Les écrits des prisonniers politiques*, thesis, Sorbonne, 1974
84. *Letters and Papers from Prison*, p. 161f.
85. Ibid., p. 419
86. Ibid., p. 168f.
87. Ibid., pp. 167, 310
88. Ibid., p. 163
89. Ibid., p. 148f.
90. Ibid., pp. 50, 125
91. GS III, p. 479f.
92. *Letters and Papers from Prison*, p. 15
93. *Honest to God*, SCM Press, London, 1963
94. GS III, p. 244f.
95. GS I, p. 145
96. Ibid., p. 26
97. Clifford Green, *The Sociality of Christ and Humanity. D. Bonhoeffer's Early Theology 1927–1933*, thesis, New York, 1971
98. GS V, Munich, 1972, p. 187
99. *Sanctorum Communio*, London, and *The Communion of Saints*, New York, 1963, p. 157
100. Karl Barth, *Church Dogmatics*, Vol. IV/2, London, 1968, p. 641
101. *Act and Being*, Collins, London and Harper & Row, New York, 1962, p. 90
102. *The Cost of Discipleship*, SCM Press, London, and Macmillan, New York, 1948, 1959, pp. 35f., 40f., 44f., 54

103. GS III, p. 25
104. *Letters and Papers from Prison*, p. 369
105. *Ethics*, Collins, London and Macmillan, New York, 1971, pp. 326–34
106. Ibid., p. 177
107. Ibid., pp. 237, 263, 265
108. Ibid., p. 109f.
109. Ibid., p. 168
110. *Letters and Papers from Prison*, pp. 380–3
111. Ibid., pp. 279–82
112. Ibid., p. 285f.
113. Ibid., p. 299f.
114. Ibid., p. 326f.
115. Ibid., pp. 344, 346
116. Ibid., p. 360f.
117. GS VI, p. 557
118. *Letters and Papers from Prison*, p. 361f.
119. Ibid., pp. 380–3
120. Ibid., p. 381f.
121. Ibid., p. 382f.
122. Ibid., pp. 281, 286, 300
123. Ibid., p. 348

Photographic Acknowledgements

The author acknowledges the use of the following photographs:
Ullstein: pp. 32, 51, 55, 64, 83, 95, 97, 100 (left), 102, 121 (upper), 126
Süddeutscher Verlag: p. 113
M. & F. Zellweger-Barth, Basle: p. 142
dpa: p. 143
Rowohlt-Archiv; p. 147
Pfarrer W. Engler, Berlin: p. 53
Karl Upisch: p. 60
Rudolf Pestalozzi, Zürich: p. 70
Pressens Bild AB, Stockholm: p. 93
From *The Steps of Bonhoeffer A Pictorial Album*, J. Martin Baily and Douglas Gilbert. United Church Press, Philadelphia: p. 117
Emmi Bonhoeffer: p. 129
All the remaining pictures are the property of the author.

Chronological Table

Life

4 February: born in Breslau, sixth out of eight children
His father, Karl Bonhoeffer, appointed to Berlin,
as neurologist

Walter Bonhoeffer, his brother, killed in France

Theological studies in Tübingen, Rome; from 1924 in Berlin

Graduation with *Sanctorum Communio* (published 1930)
Assistant pastor in Barcelona
Assistant to W. Lütgert, in the theological faculty, Berlin
July: Second theological examination, teaching qualification
with *Act and Being*
Sept.: began year of study at Union Theological Seminary,
New York

July: two weeks with Karl Barth in Bonn

Sept.: Cambridge Conference, Youth Secretary

Oct.: Student chaplain and lecturer
November: Ordination, class for confirmation candidates in
Berlin–Wedding
May: Hut in Biesenthal for students and confirmation
candidates

April: Lecture, *The Church and the Jewish Question*

May: Brother-in-Law, H. von Dohnanyi, personal consultant
to Minister of Justice

Political matters	Ecclesiastical affairs
1906	
1912	
1914 6 August: Capture of Liège	World Alliance for Friendship Between the Churches founded
1918	Karl Barth's *Epistle to the Romans*, first edition
1919 28 June: Treaty of Versailles	
1923 Nov.: 1 dollar = $2\frac{1}{2}$ billion Reichsmarks	
1925	Life and Work, Stockholm
1927	Faith and Order, Lausanne
1928	
1929 3 Oct.: Stresemann died	
1930	10 June: A. von Harnack died
Sept.: National Socialists in Reichstag increased from 12 to 107	
1931	Althaus and Hirsch, anti-ecumenical declaration
Sept.: Japan invades Manchuria Oct.: Harzburg Front Dec.: 5.7 million unemployed	
1932 30 May: Brüning's resignation	Aug.: Bell, President of Life and Work
1933 30 Jan.: Hitler Reich Chancellor March: Edict for the Protection of People and State, Treachery Law and Enabling Act	
April: Boycott of Jewish businesses and "Decree for the Reconstruction of the Professional Civil Service"	April: National Conference of "German Christians" May: Young Reformation Movement; Bodelschwingh National Bishop, June: resignation

18 July: with the Gestapo in Prinz-Albrecht-Strasse

August: Bethel Confession against the German Christians
7 Sept.: draft of points of commitment for Pastors Emergency League
27 Sept.: Protest of 2000 pastors to the Wittenberg National Synod

17 Oct.: takes up London pastorate

6 Mar.: summoned to appear before National Bishop, "free synod" in Berlin

August: co-option to the Ecumenical Council at Fanö

November: London congregations secede from Reich Church Government

April: Director of the preachers' seminary, first at Zingsthof on the Baltic
24 June: move to seminary in Finkelwalde near Stettin
Sept.: proposal for founding a "House of Brethren"

Feb.: Last Lectures in the university of Berlin

March: study visit of preachers' seminary to Denmark and Sweden

June: Controversial article on The Community of the Church

August: Forbidden by the Minister of Education to teach in the university

Political matters	Ecclesiastical affairs
20 July: Concordat with the Vatican	23 July: Church elections, about 75% German Christians; Young Reformers retire from church politics
	5 Sept.: "Brown Synod", "Aryan clause"
	27 Sept.: L. Müller, National Bishop
	13 Nov.: Krause's Sports Palace speech
1934	25 Jan.: Church leaders with Hitler
	Feb.: Heckel, National Bishop
	Apr.: Co-ordination of regional churches
	31 May: Barmen "Confessing Synod"
30 June: "Röhm-Putsch" 2 Aug.: Hindenburg's death, Hitler as President and Chancellor, "The Führer"	Aug.: Ecumenical Conference at Fanö
	20 Oct: Dahlem Confessing Synod. Proclamation of Church Emergency Law
6 Nov.: Ribbentrop visits Bell	22 Dec.: Barth dismissed from Bonn pulpit proclamation, 715 arrests
Dec.: economic disagreements with London	
1935 13 March: universal conscription	
16 July: Kerrl, Minister for Church Affairs	4 June: Augsburg Confessing Synod
15 Sept.: Nuremberg Laws	
24 Sept.: Law for the Protection of the Evangelical Church	17 Oct.: Reich Church Committee
1936	Feb.: Oeynhausen Confessing Synod Second Provisional Church Administration
7 March: remilitarization of Rhineland	28 May: Provisional Administration's memorandum to Hitler, prematurely published
July: Franco *putsch* in Morocco	23 July in *Basler Nachrichten*

Feb.: withdrawal from ecumenical ministries after London meetings

1 July: arrested during the search of Niemöller's house

October: police close the house at Finkenwalde

November: *Cost of Discipleship* published, collective pastorates in Further Pomerania
January: disruption of meeting and explusion from Berlin
February: H. von Dohnanyi with Oster in charge of the Fritsch case, first information about plans for revolt

September: *Life Together* (pub. 1939); Leibholz family emigrates

March: England, meetings with Bell, R. Niebuhr, Hodgson, Visser 't Hooft
June: a month in New York

25 Aug.: H. von Dohnanyi Supreme Commander with Canaris in Military Intelligence (*Abwehr*)
September: attempts to work as army chaplain

17 March: Gestapo closes the collective pastorate of Sigurdshof

June: first visitation in East Prussia for the Confessing Church

178

Political matters	Ecclesiastical affairs
1937 15 Feb.: Hitler's Decree for Church elections, which never took place	12 Feb.: resignation of Reich Church Committee 1 July Niemöller arrested July: Oxford Conference without Germans Dec.: preachers' seminary director, H. Iwand, arrested
Sept.: Himmler's decree against training for the Confessing Church 6 Nov: Italy in the Anti-comintern Pact 1938 4 Feb.: Fritsch crisis	
12 March: invasion and occupation of Austria	2 March: Niemöller sent to concentration camp, despite acquittal 20 April: pastors' oath to Hitler as birthday present
August: "Israel" and "Sarah" stamp in Jewish passports 29 September: Munich agreement 9 Nov.: "Crystal Night"	19 Sept.: Barth's Hromadka letter 27 Sept.: Special Prayers of the Provisional Administration on the occasion of the Sudeten crisis
1939	28 Jan.: Confessing Church synod in Nikolassee: solidarity with the "illegal" pastors
15 March: invasion of Prague, erection of Protectorate 24 Aug.: German–Soviet Pact 1 Sept.: Poland invaded 3 Sept.: England declares war 8 Nov.: Bürgerbraukeller attempt on Hitler's life 1940 Feb.: "X-Report" ready 9 April: invasion of Denmark and Norway 10 May: invasion of Benelux countries and France 17 June: capitulation of France 22 June: Compiègne	2 Sept: proclamation of "Spiritual Consultative Council for Führer and Reich" (Hymmen, Marahrens, Schultz)

14 March: Greiser's 13 points for the Churches of the Warthegau |

July: second visitation, ends with the dissolution of a study conference in Bloestau
August: third visitation, with commissions from Oster for the *Abwehr*
9 Sept.: prohibited from speaking and required to report to police in Schlawe
October: seconded to *Abwehr* office in Munich

November: guest in the Monastery of Ettal

March: first visit to Switzerland, among others to Barth and Visser 't Hooft
March: forbidden to print and publish

September: second visit to Switzerland, hints of *putsch* to Paton
October: rescue action with *Abwehr* for a number of Jews

November: severe pneumonia in Berlin

Spring: warning of post and telephone special surveillance
10–18 April: visit to Norway with Helmuth James von Moltke
10–24 May: third visit to Switzerland
30 May–2 June: meeting in Sweden with Bell; information about *putsch*
June: with the Freiburg circle of Ritter, Lampe, von Dietze, among others
July: with H. von Dohnanyi in Rome, Vatican and Venice

October: Consul Schmidhuber of the Munich *Abwehr* arrested

17 Jan.: engagement to Maria von Wedemayer

Feb.: H. von Dohnanyi in Smolensk for Tresckow's preparation for the assassination
31 March: Goethe medal for Karl Bonhoeffer on his 75th birthday
5 April: arrested with H. von Dohnanyi, J. Müller and their wives

Sept.: Battle of Britain

28 Oct.: Italy's invasion
of Greece
Nov.: scrutiny by the   19 Nov.: Grüber in
National Office for   concentration camp,
Literature   Staemmler arrested
1941 April: invasion of the   6 May: 23 members of
Balkans   the examining board of
6 June: Hitler's order for   the Confessing Church
the liquidation of the   arrested, court-proceedings
Commissars   in December
22 June: invasion of
Russia
1 Sept.: Jewish yellow
star decree
16 October: first   Dec.: Wurm's appeal for
deportation from Berlin   the work of unification:
7 Dec.: Pearl Harbor,   "To the Evangelical
U.S.A. enters war   Pastors in Germany"
1942 20 Jan.: Wannsee Con-
ference "Final solution"

4 June: attempt on
Heydrich's life
30 June: Bell reports
to Eden
23 July: Bell's telegram
of refusal
8 Nov.: Allied troops land
in North Africa
1943 14 Jan.: Casablanca,
"Unconditional
Surrender"
Feb.: end of battle for
Stalingrad
13 and 21 March:
attempts at assassination
by Tresckow,
Schlabrendorff and
Gersdorf

July: preparation of charge of "subversion of the armed forces"

Jan: Kutzner dismisses chief interrogator, Roeder, and
postpones charges

30 June: Uncle, P. von Hase, Commandant of Berlin, visits
Tegel prison

October: Klaus Bonhoeffer, Rüdiger Schleicher and E. Bethge
arrested
8 October.: transferred to Gestapo cellar in Prinz-Albrecht-Strasse

7 February: sent to Buchenwald, from 3 April moved further
east
9 April: hanged in Flossenbürg with Canaris, Oster and others,
H. von Dohnanyi killed in Sachsenhausen
23 April: Klaus Bonhoeffer and Rüdiger Schleicher murdered

Political matters	*Ecclesiastical affairs*
25 July: Badoglio's *coup d'état* Sept.: Himmler, Minister of the Interior 1944 Feb.: Canaris suspended, *Abwehr* incorporated into RHSA (Head Office for national security) 6 June: Allied landings in Normandy 20 July: Stauffenberg's attempt at assassination 22 Sept.: discovery of Zossen documents	16 October.: last Confessing Synod in Breslau, declaration on the fifth order, against the murder of non-Aryans and "useless lives"
1945 5 April: order for the annihilation of the Canaris group given to Huppenkothen at Hitler's midday conference 30 April: Hitler's suicide	

Testimonies

WILLEM ADOLF VISSER 'T HOOFT
(*on his first meeting with Bonhoeffer in March 1939*)

We had heard a great deal about each other, but it was surprising how quickly we were able to get beyond the first stage of merely feeling our way, into the more intimate areas of real talks – so that, in fact, he was soon treating me as an old friend ... He described the situation of his church and country. He spoke in a way that was remarkably free from illusions, and sometimes almost clairvoyant, about the coming war, which would start soon, probably in the summer, and which would cause the Confessing Church to be forced into even greater distress ... Had not the time now come to refuse to serve a government that was heading for war and breaking all the Commandments? But what would be the consequences of such an attitude on the part of the Confessing Church? I remember his acute questions better than his answers; but I think I learnt more from his questions than he did from my answers. In the impenetrable world between "Munich" and "Warsaw", in which hardly anyone ventured to formulate the actual problems clearly, that questioning voice was a release.

(Written in 1945)

PAYNE BEST
(*English officer, fellow prisoner in Buchenwald in 1945*)

He was cheerful and ready to join in any joke. Bonhoeffer was all humility and sweetness; he always seemed to diffuse an atmosphere of happiness, of joy in every smallest event in life, and of deep gratitude for the mere fact that he was alive ... He was one of the very few men I have ever met to whom his God was real and ever close to him.

PAUL LEHMANN
(*Professor of Theology and Bonhoeffer's friend in the USA*)

His aristocracy was unmistakable yet not obtrusive, chiefly, I think, owing to his boundless curiosity about every new environment in which he found himself and to his irresistible and unfailing sense of humour. Thus he could suggest without offence that we should not play tennis

184

together since he commanded a certain expertness at the game which I could not claim . . . This curiosity about the new and different, this unfailing humour . . . always turned the incongruity between human aspiration and human failing away from human hurt to the enrichment of comradeship . . . the capacity to see oneself and the world from a perspective other than one's own. This paradox of birth and nationality in Bonhoeffer has seemed to me increasingly during the years since to have made him an exciting and conspicuous example of the triumph over parochialism of every kind.

REINHOLD NIEBUHR

Bonhoeffer's story is worth recording. It is part of the modern Acts of the Apostles . . . Despite his youthfulness – when he died, he was only in his thirties – he was one of the most influential leaders of the Church's resistance in Germany. He was certainly the most uncompromising and the bravest of them . . . He was a brilliant young theologian, combining deep piety with a high degree of intellectual refinement.

It is safe to predict that his life and his death will become one of the sources of grace for a new Church in a new Germany. We had thought that his life would be spared for the work of the Church after the war . . . Bonhoeffer held remarkably clear religious views and at the same time the purity of a completely dedicated soul. When we recall how short a time he had to develop political and social interests, his acute appreciation of political and military devlopments is seen to be particularly remarkable . . .

Less well known than Niemöller at the present time, Bonhoeffer will one day be much more famous. Not only his martyrdom, but also his deeds and projects contain the hope of a new revival of Protestant faith in Germany. It will be a deeper faith than that of many of its critics. It will have enabled people to learn to overcome the one disastrous mistake of German Protestantism: that is, the complete separation of faith from political life.

June 1945

GEORGE BELL
(*Bishop of Chichester*)

I knew him in London in the early days of the evil regime: and from him, more than from any other German, I learned the true character of the conflict, in an intimate friendship. I have no doubt that he did fine work with his German congregation: but he taught many besides his fellow-countrymen while a pastor in England. He was crystal clear in his convictions: and young as he was, and humble-minded as he was, he saw the truth, and spoke it with a complete absence of fear.

(Preface to *The Cost of Discipleship*, 1948)

HARVEY COX

Naturally Bonhoeffer has been misunderstood and misused. And that will happen again! Naturally, individualistic theological qualities are dangerous! But we are in no way finished with Bonhoeffer. I also do not believe that we can move on beyond him, until we can begin to become the kind of Church that according to him we must become; namely a Church which lives on the frontiers of unbelief, which aims at and speaks specifically to our time, which no longer fashions the message and mission to suit its own comfort, but for the health and for the renewal of the world.

1965

KARL BARTH
(*to Eberhard Bethge*)

In Germany, encumbered as it was by the problems of its Lutheran tradition, there arose a "pent-up demand" in an area that I had passed over in silence or given very little attention: ethics – co-humanity – the serving Church – discipleship – socialism – the peace movement – and in it all and with it all, inevitably, politics. This gap, this lack, was what Bonhoeffer felt needed filling from the outset, with increasing urgency, and he expressed it in broad terms. And his long-overdue completion of my thought, which he undertook with such force and, I hope, finality, holds the secret of the impression which he rightly made and still makes, especially since it is on these very points that he became a martyr.

22 May 1967

DMITRIJ M. UGRINOVICH
(*Professor of dialectical and historical Materialism, Moscow*)

An important and original figure among the Protestant theologians with a "social" tendency was the German Lutheran pastor and theologian, Dietrich Bonhoeffer. His personal destiny and that of his ideas were in no way ordinary . . . Bonhoeffer trod his own path, independent of his spiritual forefathers. From the beginning his real interest was not in dogmatic and specifically religious problems but rather in social ones . . .

Bonhoeffer introduced into theological literature the concept of the world's coming of age . . .

It is not difficult to see how Bonhoeffer rejects all the fundamental tenets of traditional Christian doctrine. The Christian presentation of

186

God, of the supernatural in the other world, is subjected by him to a severe and in many respects justified criticism . . .

If we disregard some of Bonhoeffer's vague religious ideas which are of no great interest to us, such as that of the Christian God who is a God of suffering in sympathy with the sufferings of men, in contrast with the gods of other religions that seem to men to be alien and powerful beings, then Bonhoeffer sees the essence of Christian doctrine in the evangelical teaching of love of man's neighbour . . . Bonhoeffer's ethical views bear a social and activist stamp . . .

So for Bonhoeffer the essence of Christianity lies not in a recognition of God, nor in a belief in him as the creator of the world, but in the realization of the Christian ethic in human behaviour.

1968

JAMES MARK

Without the letters to Bethge he would be a heroic figure in the history of the Confessing Church but, as a writer, an interesting young theologian whose promise had never been fulfilled. It would be difficult to say even what form that fulfilment might have taken. What happened to him in the last phase of his life is at once a tragedy and a priceless and providential gift to the whole Church, wherever its boundaries may be drawn. These letters and papers offer us the most significant and seminal theological insights of our time. That one can say this of something so brief and fragmentary is itself significant. He was exploring – really exploring – the possibilities of theology at the frontiers of contemporary experience.

1973

Bibliography

Works by Dietrich Bonhoeffer
available in English

Act and Being (*Akt und Sein*), E.T., Collins, London and Harper & Row, New York, 1962

Christology (title in USA: *Christ the Center*), Collins/Fount Paperbacks, London and Harper & Row, New York, new translation, 1978

The Cost of Discipleship (*Nachfolge*), E.T., S.C.M. Press, London and Macmillan, New York, 1959

Creation and Fall (*Schöpfung und Fall*), E.T., S.C.M. Press, London and Macmillan, New York, 1959

Ethics (*Ethik*), E.T., Collins/Fontana, London and Macmillan, New York, 1964

Letters and Papers From Prison (*Widerstand und Ergebung*), E.T., Enlarged Edition, S.C.M. Press, London and Macmillan, New York, 1971

Prayers From Prison (*Von Guten Mächten: Gebete und Gedichte, interpretiert von Johann Christoph Hampe*), E.T., Collins, London and Fortress Press, Philadelphia, 1977

Sanctorum Communio (title in USA: *The Communion of Saints*), E.T., Collins, London and Harper & Row, New York, 1963

The Collected Works of Dietrich Bonhoeffer (*Gesammelte Schriften*), E.T., selections from the German, in three volumes:

1. *No Rusty Swords* (1928–36)
2. *The Way to Freedom* (1935–39)
3. *True Patriotism* (1939–45)

Collins, London and Harper & Row, New York, 1965, 1966 and 1966 respectively

Index of Names

The figures given in italics denote photographs

INDEX

INDEX